This book

belongs

to

Hold this page up to a mirror and then write your names below
(make sure the writing is back-to-front, too).

and

First edition for the United States, its territories and
possessions, and Canada published in 2015 by

Barron's Educational Series, Inc.

Copyright © 2014 Ivy Press Limited

This book was conceived, designed & produced by

Ivy Press
210 High Street
Lewes
East Sussex BN7 2NS
United Kingdom
www.ivypress.co.uk

All inquiries should be addressed to:
Barron's Educational Series, Inc.
250 Wireless Boulevard, Hauppauge, New York 11788
www.barronseduc.com

ISBN: 978-1-4380-0605-5

Ivy Press

CREATIVE DIRECTOR   Peter Bridgewater
COMMISSIONING EDITOR   Georgia Amson-Bradshaw
MANAGING EDITOR   Hazel Songhurst
PROJECT EDITOR   Jacqui Sayers
ART DIRECTOR   Kim Hankinson
DESIGNER & ILLUSTRATOR   Lydia Crook

Product conforms to all applicable CPSC and CPSIA 2008
standards. No lead or phthalate hazards.

Manufactured by: 1010 Printing, Guangdong, China
Date of manufacture: December 2014

9 8 7 6 5 4 3 2 1

Lydia Crook

TWO PLAYER BIG FUN BOOK

BARRON'S

HOW TO USE THIS BOOK

The Two Player Big Fun Book is packed with fun things for a pair of pals.

For some activities, you will work together as a team. For others, you are in competition!

Fun this **BIG** can't all fit in the same way up as a normal book, though. You'll need to move the book around and change where you're sitting for each activity—depending on which way is up for the text.

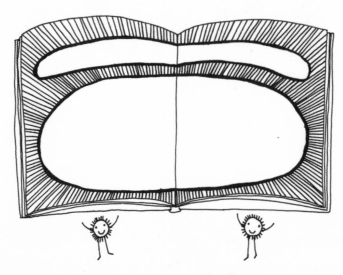

Sometimes you'll sit beside each other . . .

... other times you'll sit opposite each other, with the book in between.

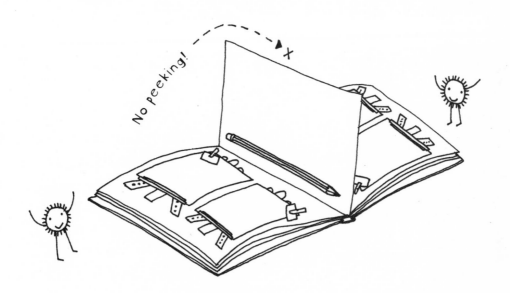

Some activities have a "screen" page for you to hold up in the middle. This is to prevent peeking while the game is underway!

Most of the games appear more than once. Take turns going first, so you both have the chance to do everything and get an equal share of the Big Fun.

Woo hoo!

THE FIEND

How to play the fiendish maze ...
Face each other at opposite sides of the book. See which player can get through the maze on the page to reach the center first.

PLAY
SQUARES
ON THIS PAGE

→

How to play . . .

Take turns drawing a single line to join any two dots that are next to each other on the grid. The lines can join the dots horizontally or vertically (but not diagonally).

The player whose line completes one square earns one point, and puts his or her initials in that square. This player then gets another turn.

The game ends when no more lines can be drawn. The player with the most points wins!

The steps below show one square being drawn. Player "B" drew the final line in the square and receives that point.

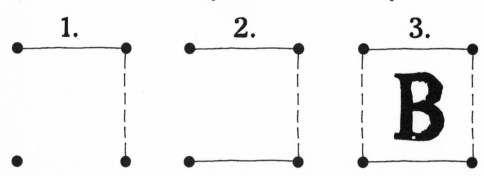

—— Player A   - - - Player B

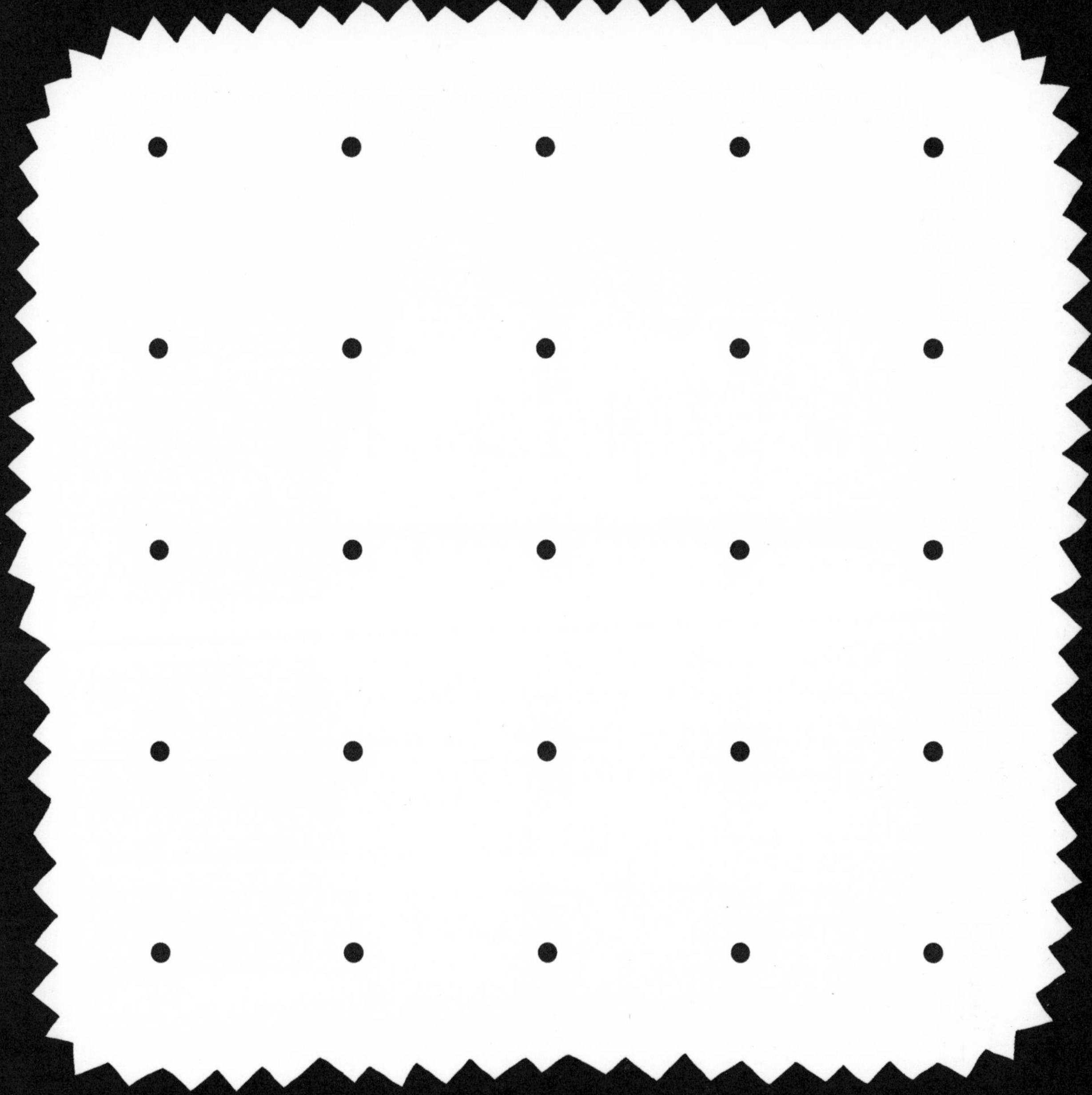

PLAYER 1 STATS

Name _____

Age _____

Number of squares won

_____

PLAYER 2 STATS

Name _____

Age _____

Number of squares won

_____

The winner was _____ with ___ squares.

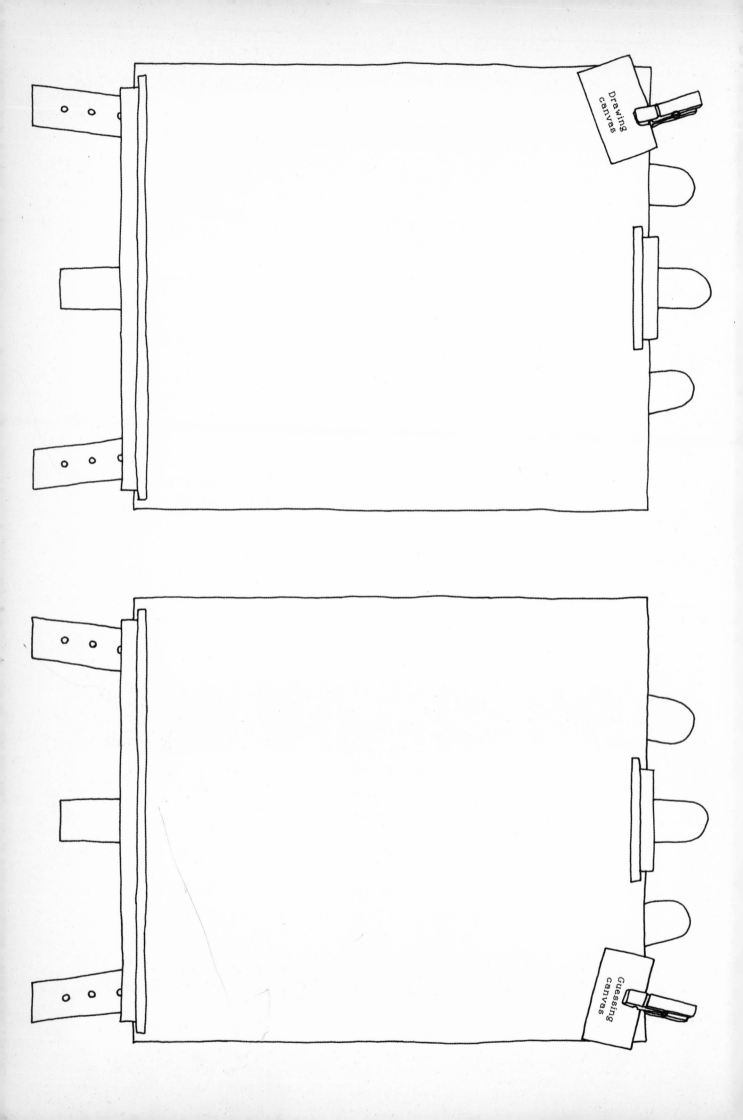

SAY WHAT YOU SEE

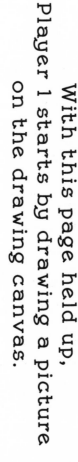

With this page held up, Player 1 starts by drawing a picture on the drawing canvas.

Good work—but now the hard part!

Describe the shapes and lines that make up your picture, without saying what you have drawn. For example, if you drew a house, you could describe it as a square with a triangle on top. Player 2 must try drawing a copy of it on the guessing canvas, just from the description.

No questions, and no guessing until the end!

Once you've finished, trade roles, so you both have a turn at drawing and at guessing.

SAY WHAT YOU SEE?

With this page held up,
Player 1 starts by drawing a picture
on the drawing canvas.

Good work—but now the hard part!

Describe the shapes and lines that make up your picture,
without saying what you have drawn. For example, if you drew
a house, you could describe it as a square with a triangle on top.
Player 2 must try drawing a copy of it on the guessing canvas, just
from the description.

No questions, and no guessing until the end!

Once you've finished, trade roles, so you both have a
turn at drawing and at guessing.

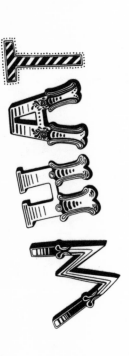

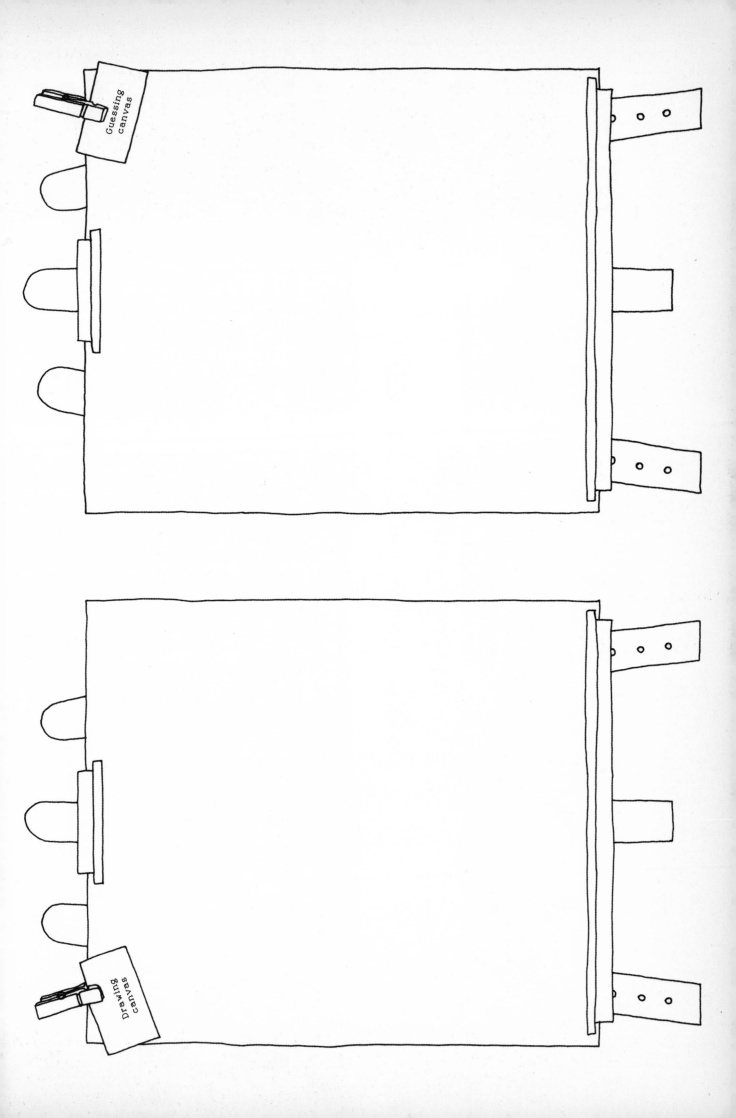

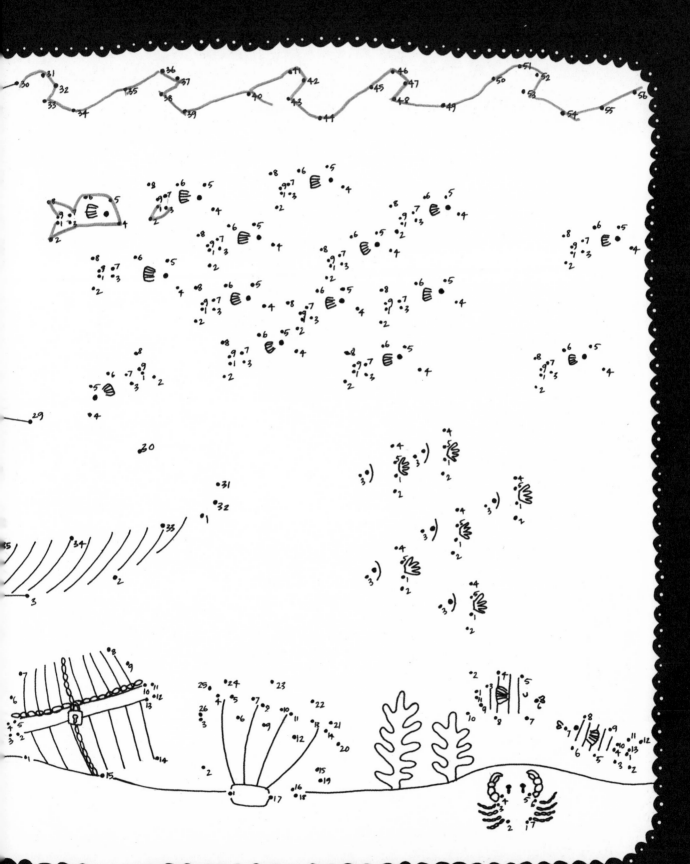

WHAT'S THE STORY?

PLAYER 1'S STORY

1 " .... !!" she shouted, while she

2 .... the 3 ....

She was taking her 4 .... pet

5 .... to the vet because he had a sore

6 .... , but her car had broken down

on the way, so they both had to

7 .... there, 8 ....
....

WORD KEY:

1. Exclamation!   3. Noun   5. Noun   7. Verb
2. Verb (past tense)   4. Adjective   6. Noun   8. Adverb (ending ... ly)

Read through your story (silently!) and ask the other player for words to fill in the blanks (clues on the types of words you need are provided). Once you've both filled in all the gaps, take turns reading your story aloud to see whose is the funniest.

PLAYER 2'S STORY

Wesley was learning to play the 1 ...., but was progressing 2 .... because he had to use his 3 .... Sometimes his pet 4 .... tried to help, but wasn't very good because its fur was too 5 .... After lots of time spent 6 ...., they both felt 7 .... with their 8 ....

WORD KEY:

1. Noun
2. Adverb (ending ...ly)
3. Noun
4. Noun
5. Adjective
6. Verb (ending ....ing)
7. Noun (emotion)
8. Noun

MANDALA DRAWING

Mandalas are beautiful, detailed patterns and you can create two here. They've been started for you. You can both draw at the same time—add something to your own pattern, then switch sides and add something to the other. You could draw a decorative ring each time and add dots, shapes, swirls, squiggles—anything you like!

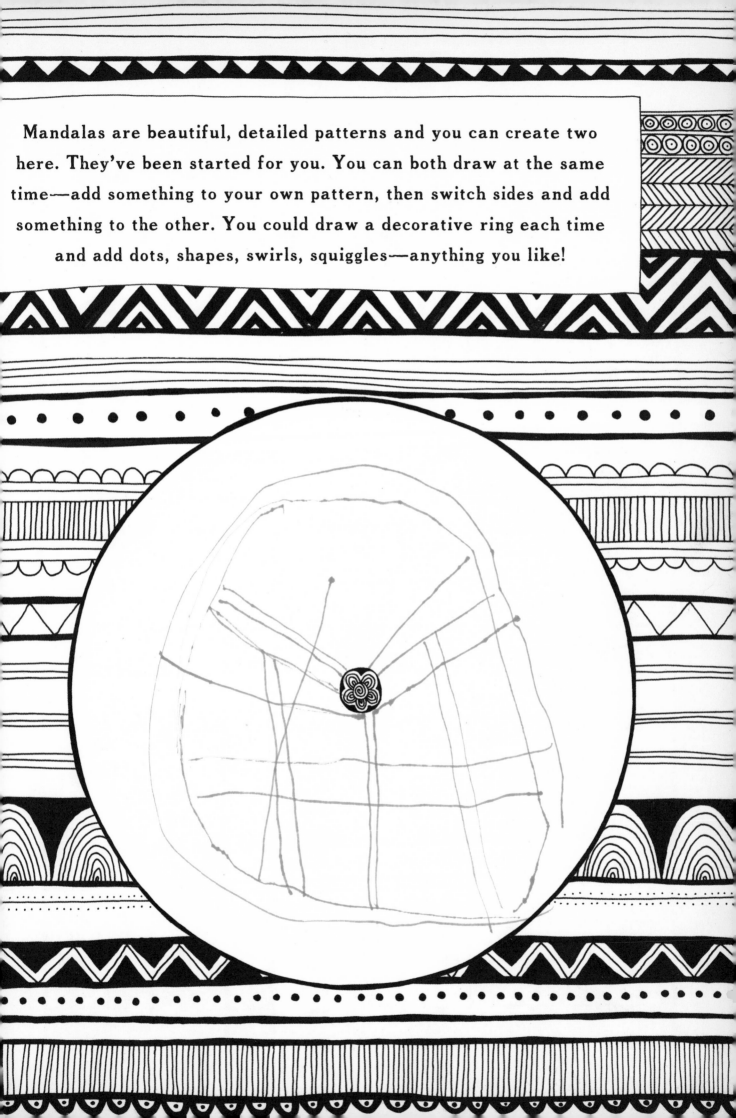

MAIN GRID

Draw your fleet on this grid.

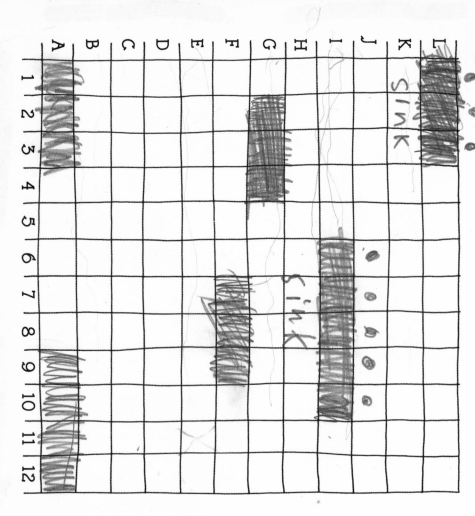

sink

sink

sink

TRACKING GRID

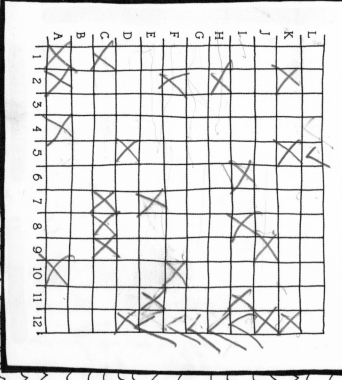

YOUR FLEET

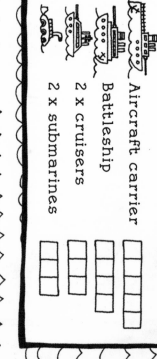

Aircraft carrier

Battleship

2 x cruisers

2 x submarines

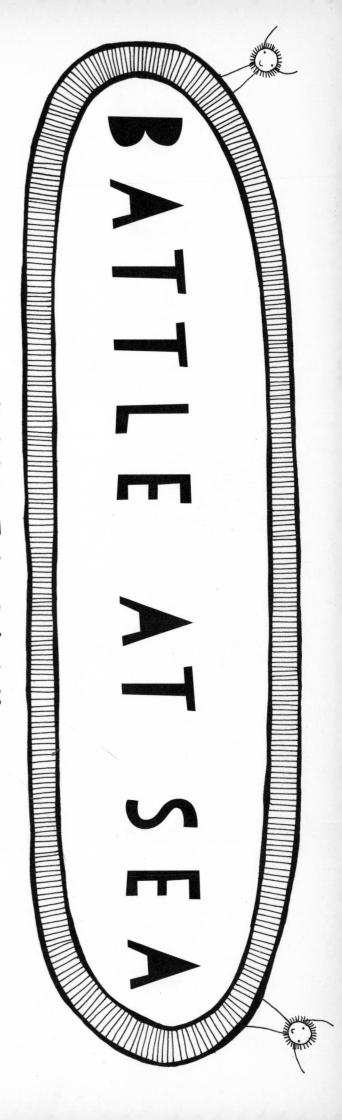

BATTLE AT SEA

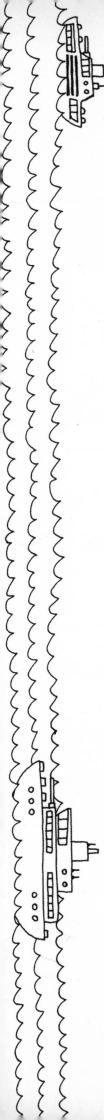

HOW TO PLAY . . .

Sit facing each other, then hold this page up in the middle.

Choose where you want to place each boat in your fleet. Shade in the correct number of squares on the main grid for each boat, then you're ready to play.

Take turns calling out a square from the grid (A3, D5, etc.). The other player then checks the grid and tells you if they have a boat on that square. If the answer is yes—you've got a hit! Mark hits with a cross on your tracking grid, and mark misses with a dash. This will help you build a picture of where the other player's fleet is located.

Once you've guessed all of the squares taken up by one boat, you have sunk that boat! When all of one player's boats have been sunk, the other player has WON THE BATTLE!

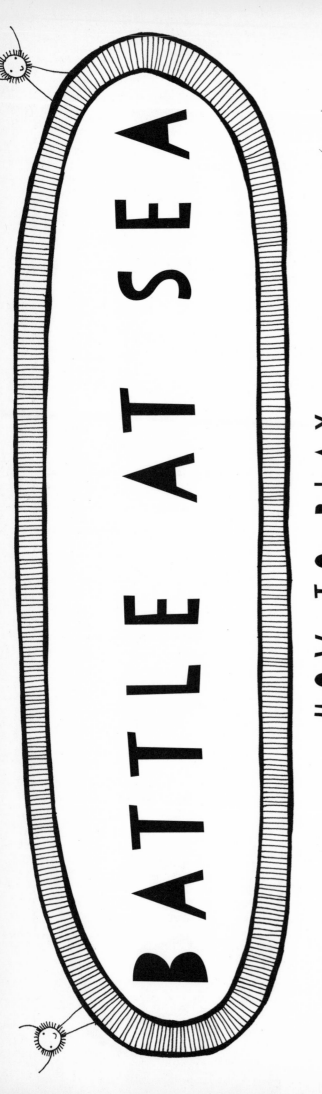

BATTLE AT SEA

HOW TO PLAY . . .

Sit facing each other, then hold this page up in the middle.

Choose where you want to place each boat in your fleet. Shade in the correct number of squares on the main grid for each boat, then you're ready to play.

Take turns calling out a square from the grid (A3, D5, etc.). The other player then checks the grid and tells you if they have a boat on that square. If the answer is yes—you've got a hit! Mark hits with a cross on your tracking grid, and mark misses with a dash. This will help you build a picture of where the other player's fleet is located.

Once you've guessed all of the squares taken up by one boat, you have sunk that boat! When all of one player's boats have been sunk, the the other player has WON THE BATTLE!

YOUR FLEET

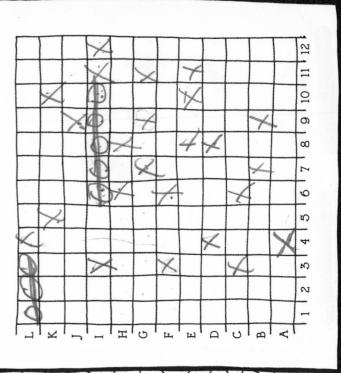

- Aircraft carrier
- Battleship
- 2 x cruisers
- 2 x submarines

TRACKING GRID

MAIN GRID

Draw your fleet on this grid.

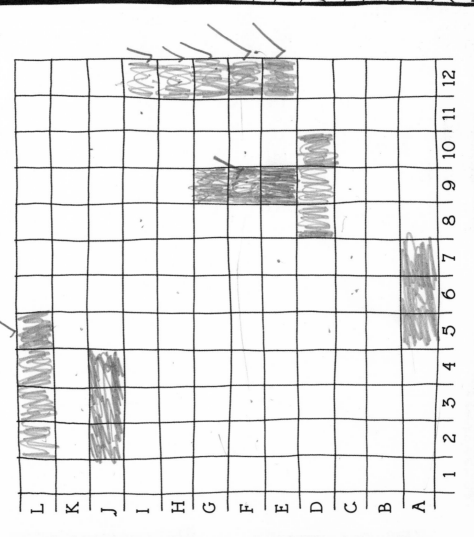

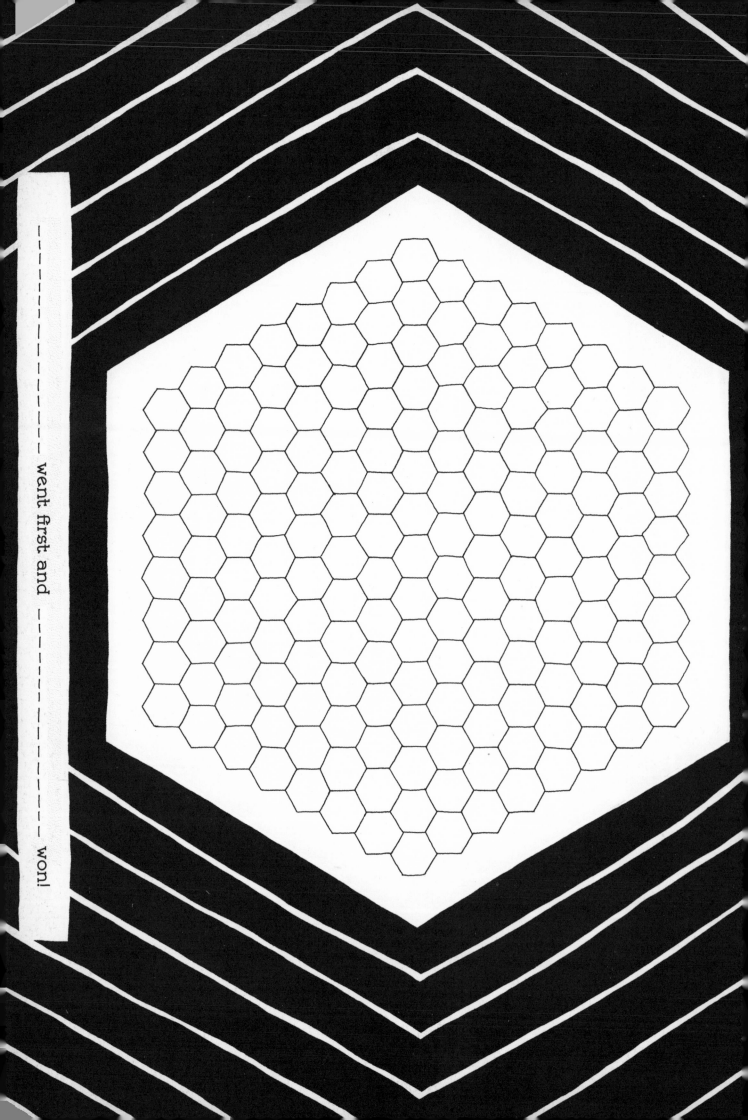

went first and ——— won!

HEXAGONS

HOW TO PLAY . . .

Each player should choose a colored pencil to use for the game.
Take turns filling in one "cell" of the board at a time with your color.

The goal is to color cells next to each other to create one of
these three connections:

1. A ring, which is a continuous loop with at least one cell in the middle.

2. A fork, which connects three edges of the board (the corners don't count as an edge).

3. A bridge, which connects any two of the corners.

The first player to make any of these connections wins!

MY SCORE WAS:

MY LIST OF WORDS FOUND:

HOW TO PLAY:

With this page held up, the first player calls out a letter, then both players write that letter in a square on their grid. Take turns calling out letters and writing them down until both grids are full. The goal is to arrange the letters as you write them down to make as many words as possible.

Once the grids are full, write down all the words you can find. You get points for words in a vertical or horizontal row (not diagonals). You also get points for words within words—so if you found "train," you'd also get points for "rain" and "in."

5-letter word—Wow, well done! 10 points!
4-letter word—Good effort, 5 points.
3-letter word—Not bad, 2 points.
2-letter word—OK, you can have 1 point.

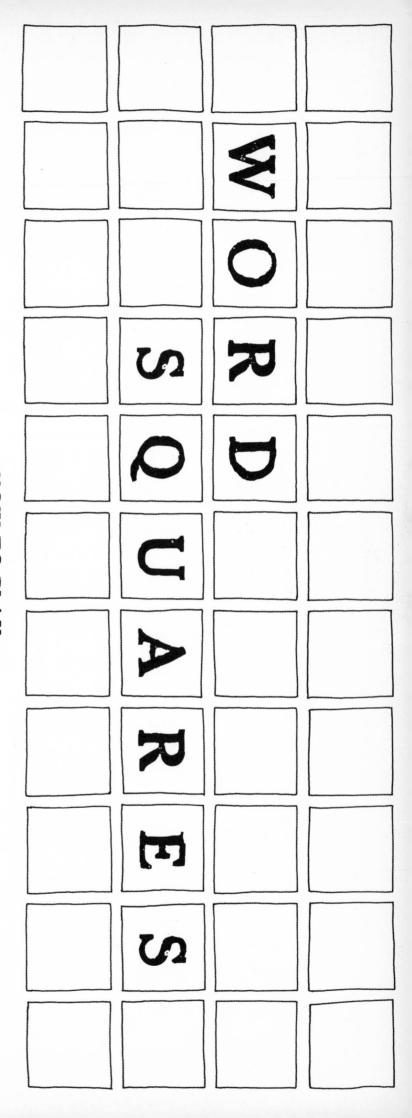

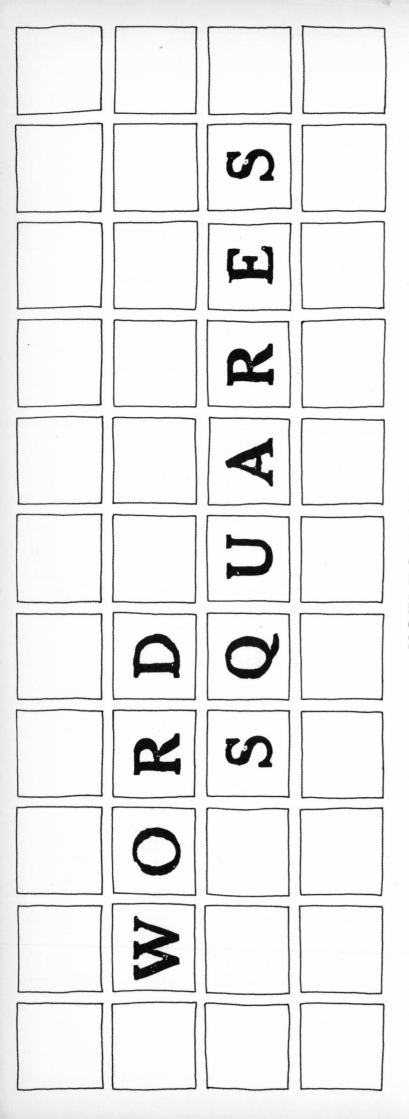

HOW TO PLAY:

With this page held up, the first player calls out a letter, then both players write that letter in a square on the grid. Take turns calling out letters and writing them down until both grids are full. The goal is to arrange the letters as you write them down to make as many words as possible.

Once the grids are full, write down all the words you can find.

You get points for words in a vertical or horizontal row (not diagonals). You also get points for words within words—so if you found "train," you'd also get points for "rain" and "in."

5-letter word—Wow, well done! 10 points!

4-letter word—Good effort, 5 points.

3-letter word—Not bad, 2 points.

2-letter word—OK, you can have 1 point.

MY LIST OF WORDS FOUND:

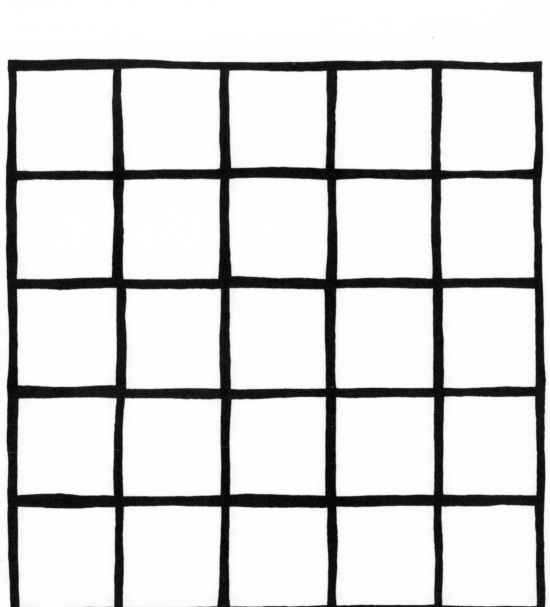

MY SCORE WAS:

Sometimes, starting a drawing is the hardest part. Luckily, you can help each other out! Each player should quickly do a small squiggle in the middle of the frame, then turn the book around.

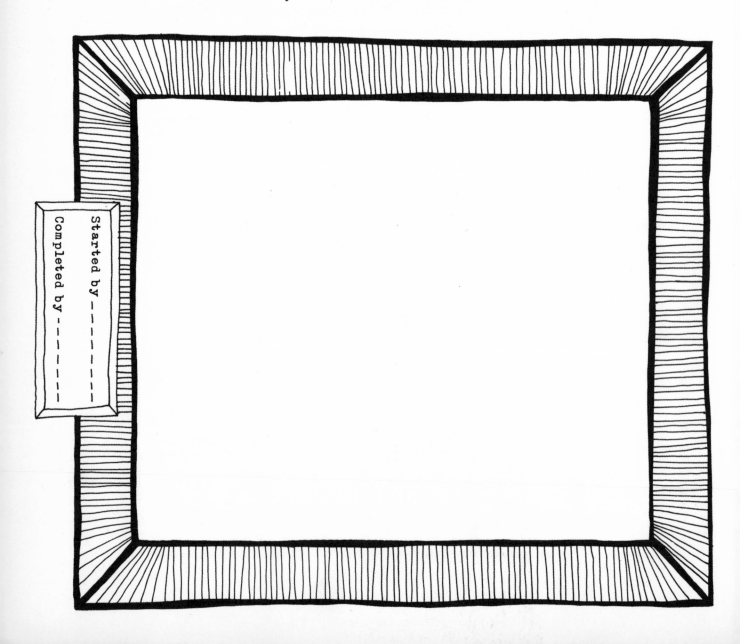

Started by _ _ _ _ _ _ _

Completed by _ _ _ _ _ _ _

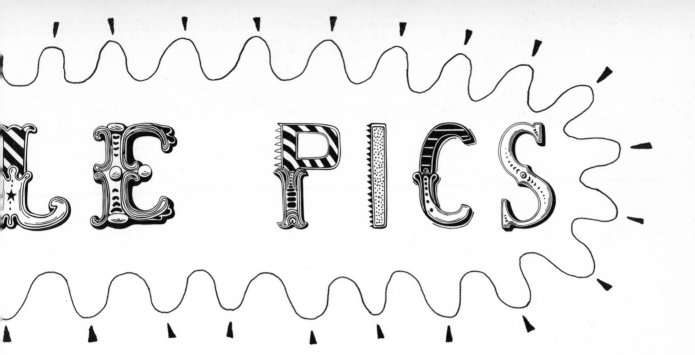

Now that the drawing has been started for you, decide what you think it looks like and add details to turn it into a complete picture!

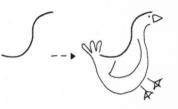

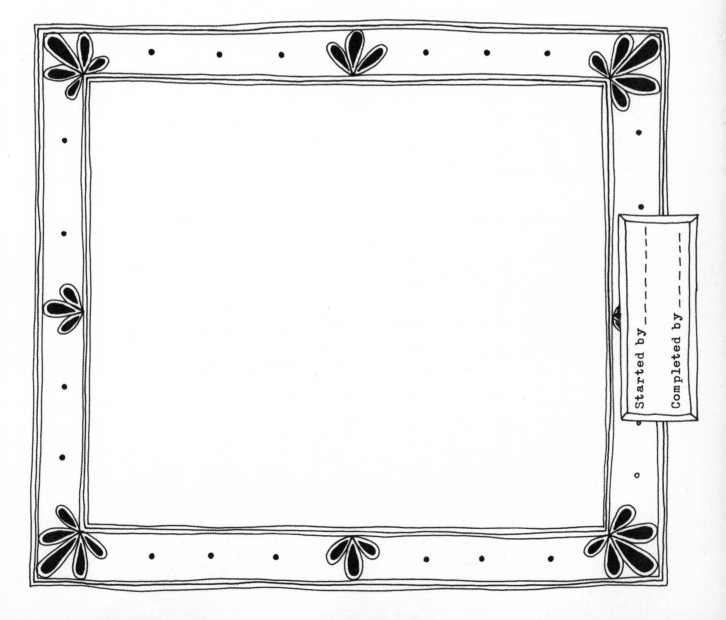

Started by _ _ _ _ _ _ _

Completed by _ _ _ _ _ _ _

	FRUITS	ANIMALS	COUNTRIES	CARTOONS	MOVIES
G					
L					
O					
V					
E					

MY TOTAL CATEGORIES SCORE WAS: _____

CATEGORIES

How does it work?

Hold up this page and set a timer for four minutes—you're ready to start!

In each square of the grid, write a word that fits under the category at the top of the column, and starts with the letter at the beginning of the row.

The game is finished when the time is up or when one player completely fills the grid.

Compare your answers and make sure you agree all the words are OK (no made-up words!).

You get no points for words that both you and the other player wrote down, but one point per word that only you thought of. If you filled the whole grid, you get five bonus points!

The player with the most points wins.

Ready, set, go . . .

CATEGORIES

How does it work?

Hold up this page and set a timer for four minutes—you're ready to start!

In each square of the grid, write a word that fits under the category at the top of the column, and starts with the letter at the beginning of the row.

The game is finished when the time is up or when one player completely fills the grid.

Compare your answers and make sure you agree all the words are OK (no made-up words!).

You get no points for words that both you and the other player wrote down, but one point per word that only you thought of. If you filled the whole grid, you get five bonus points!

The player with the most points wins.

Ready, set, go . . . . .

	FRUITS	ANIMALS	COUNTRIES	CARTOONS	MOVIES
G					
L					
O					
V					
E					

MY TOTAL CATEGORIES SCORE WAS: _ _ _ _ _

TAG-TEAM DRAWING

Work together to create a unique masterpiece, with this game of tag-team drawing . . . Player 1 does a quick doodle, then rotates the paper 90 degrees. Now it's Player 2's turn. "TAG!" Player 2 quickly adds to the doodle, then rotates the paper another 90 degrees. Keep taking turns until the picture is complete—voila!

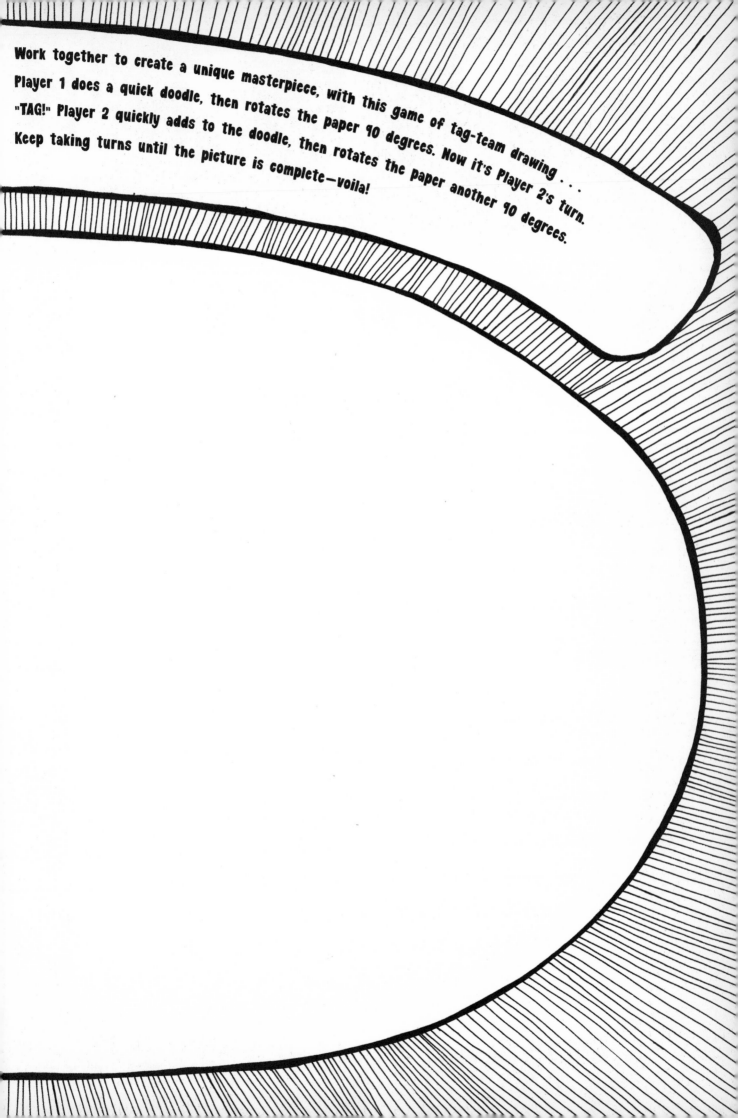

P I P E

HOW TO PLAY:

One player plays with black dots, the other plays with white dots.

Take turns connecting the dots, one line at a time. You can connect up or across (not diagonally), and you can only connect dots of your own color. You cannot cross a line that has already been drawn.

The goal is to connect the dots in your color to make a continuous line (or pipe) between the shorter sides of the grid.

LAYER

- ● Black dot player's name _ _ _ _ _ _ _ _ _ _ _ _ _ _ _ _
- ○ White dot player's name _ _ _ _ _ _ _ _ _ _ _ _ _ _ _

◄ _ _ _ _ _ White dot player joins side to side _ _ ►

Black dot player joins up or down

The winner was _ _ _ _ _ _ _ _ _ _ _ _ _ _ _ _

SPOT THE DIFFERENCE RACE

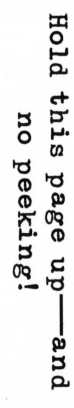

Race each other to find the ten differences between these pictures—circle them as you find them. The first player to find all ten, wins.

Hold this page up—and no peeking!

SPOT THE DIFFERENCES RACE

Race each other to find the ten differences between these pictures—circle them as you find them. The first player to find all ten, wins.

Hold this page up—and no peeking!

PICTURE

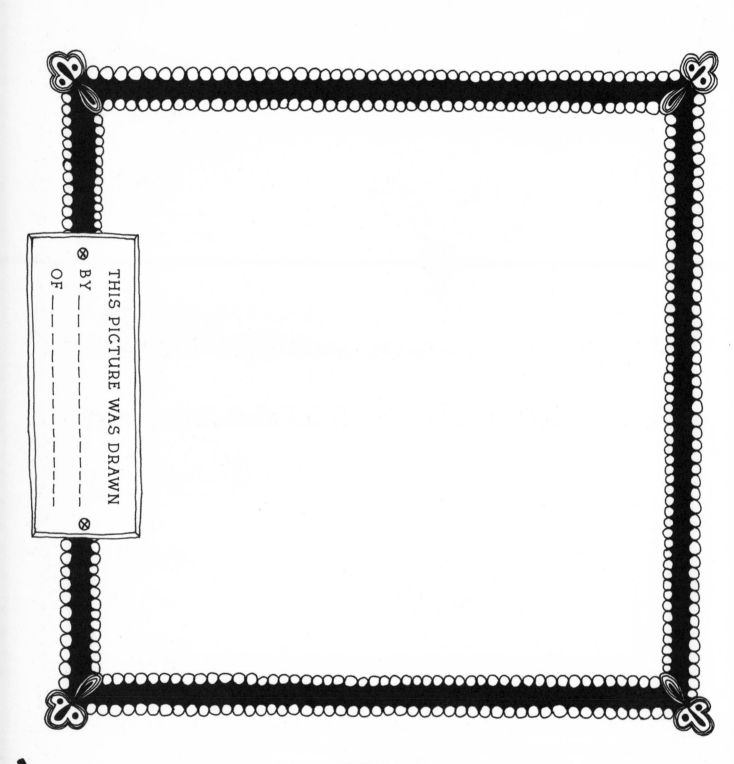

THIS PICTURE WAS DRAWN

⊗ BY
_ _ _ _ _ _ _ _ _ _ _

OF
_ _ _ _ _ _ _ _ _ _ _
_ _ _ _ _ _ _ _ _ _ _

⊗

THE GAME
Sitting at opposite ends of the book, draw a portrait of each other
in the picture frame. Sounds easy enough, right?
WELL, there is a twist...
You must NOT look down at your drawing, you can ONLY look
straight ahead at the person you are drawing!!

PERFECT

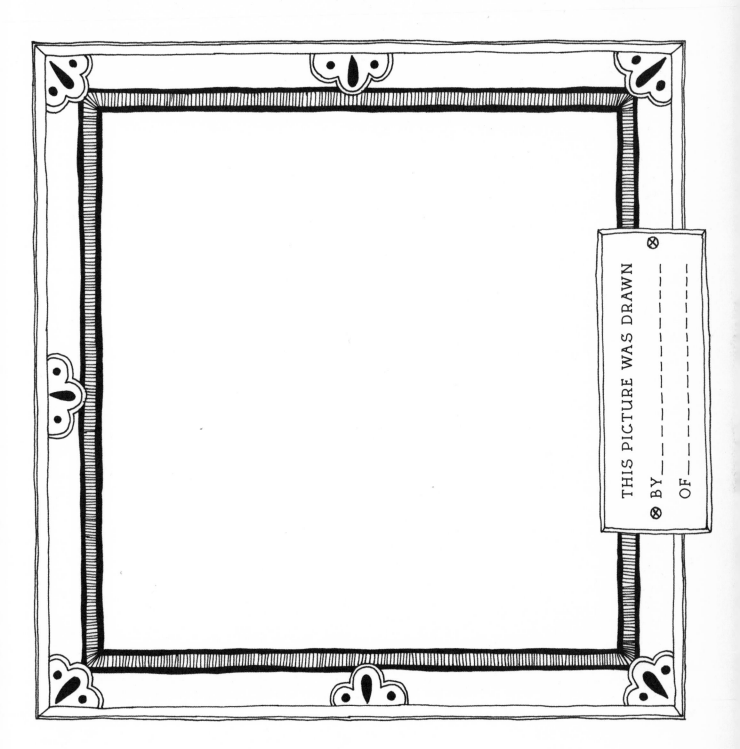

THIS PICTURE WAS DRAWN

BY _ _ _ _ _ _ _ _ _ _

OF _ _ _ _ _ _ _ _ _ _

When you have finished you can look at your portraits. Beautiful!
Optional Rule: Make it doubly exciting by playing against the clock.
Try to complete your portraits in 30 seconds!

SPROUTS

Sprouts is like a game of dot-to-dot, but with a twist . . . .

 Here's how it works:

Starting with the three dots on the opposite page, take turns drawing a line to connect two dots (or the line may start and end on the same dot). You should also draw a new dot somewhere on the new line.

Lines cannot cross, and each dot can only have three lines sprouting out of it. Eventually, it will become impossible to draw a new line without crossing an existing one—the last player to draw a line wins!

Here's an example of a two dot game :

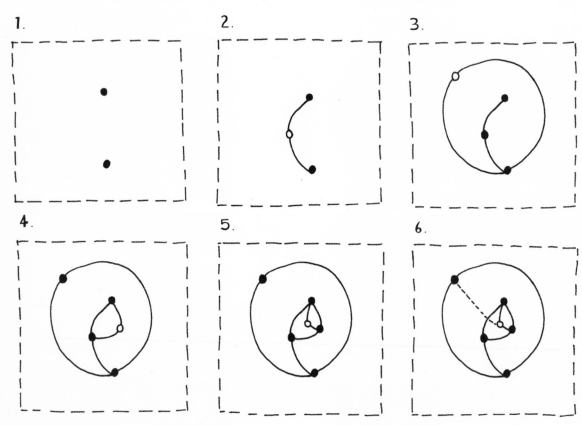

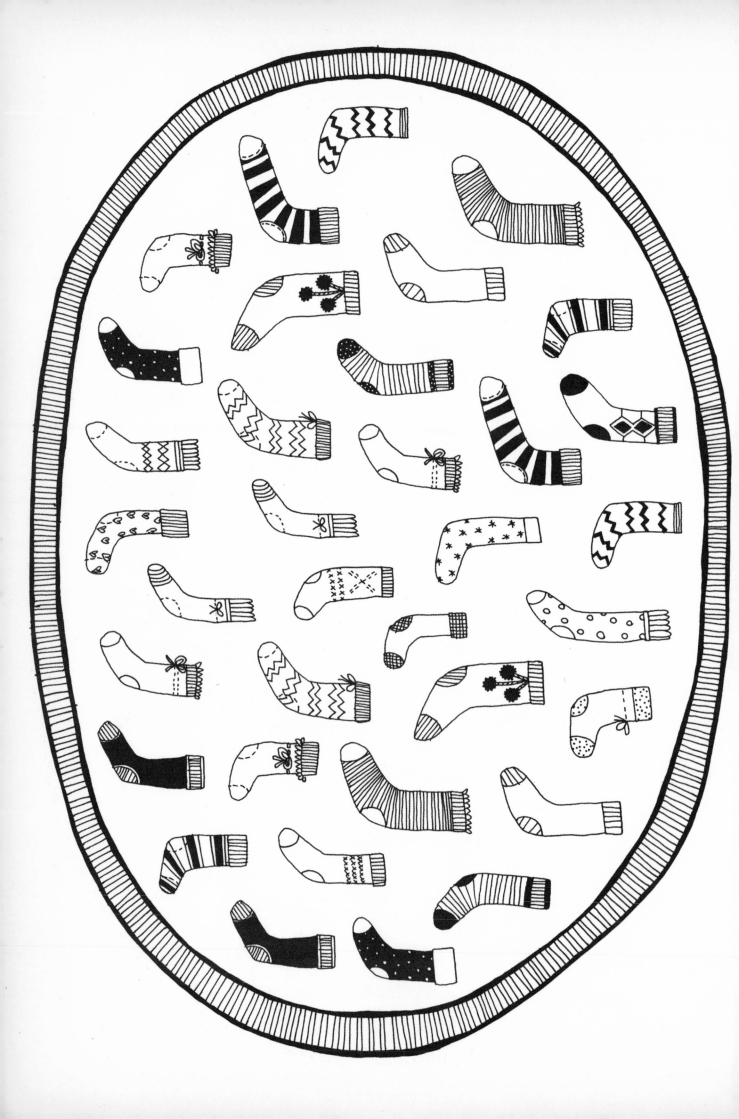

FIND THE PAIRS RACE

How it works:

Hidden in this scene are 13 pairs of identical socks.
Starting at the same time, try to find the pairs
and draw a line connecting them as you
go—the first to find all 13, wins!

Hold up this page.

FIND THE PAIRS RACE

How it works:

Hidden in this scene are 13 pairs of identical socks.

Starting at the same time, try to find the pairs

and draw a line connecting them as you

go—the first to find all 13, wins!

Hold up this page

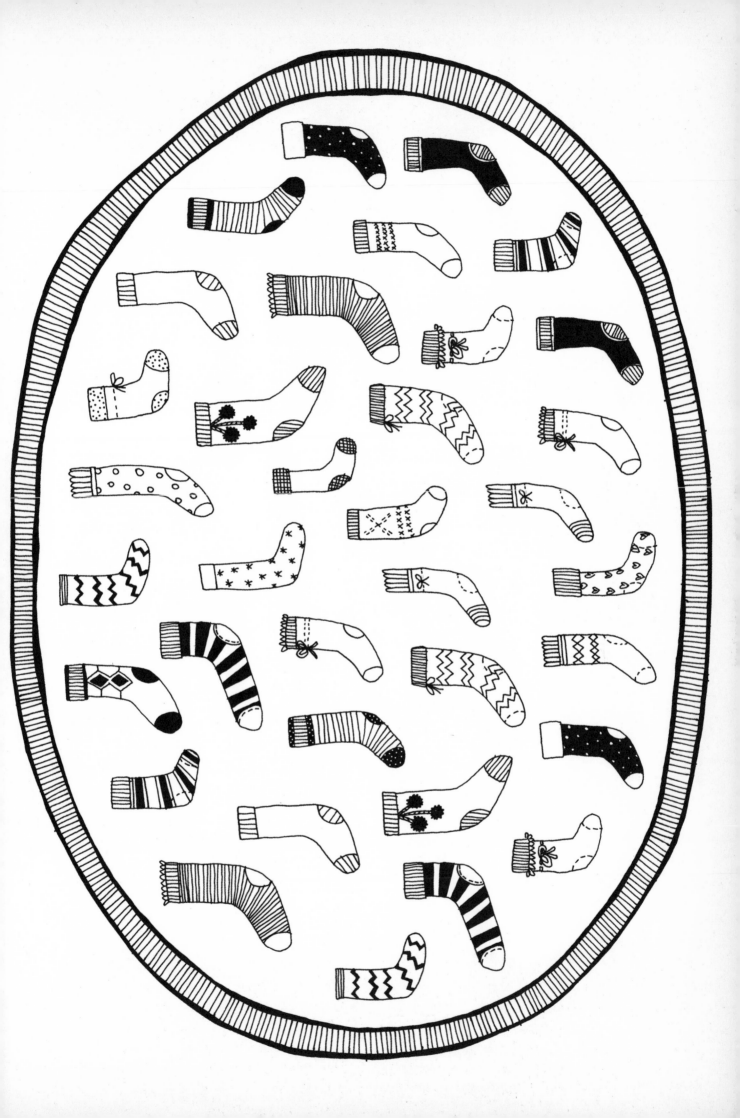

MIRROR DRAWING

drew this picture

WHAT TO DO:
Facing each other, pick one player to be lead artist and one to be the
student. The artist begins drawing a beautiful scene in the picture
frame. The student must try to mirror what the lead artist is drawing—

_____ drew this picture

WHAT TO DO:

Facing each other, pick one player to be lead artist and one to be the student. The artist begins drawing a beautiful scene in the picture frame. The student must try to mirror what the lead artist is drawing—

FINGER

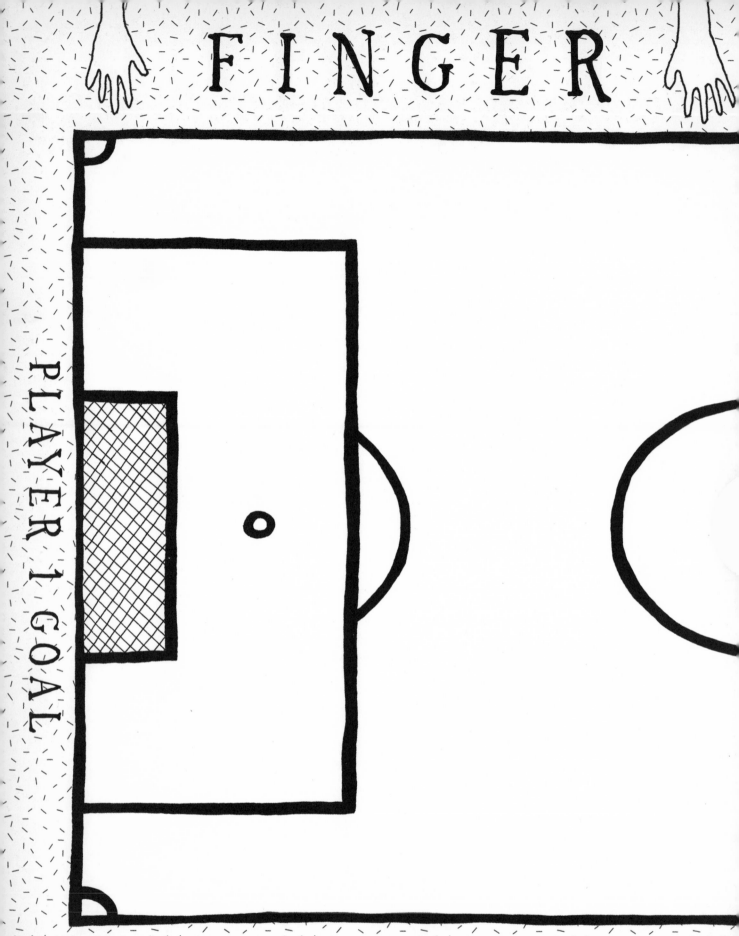

PLAYER 1 GOAL

PENALTY SHOOT-OUT

Make a soccer ball with a crumpled up piece of paper; old receipts are perfect.
Take turns placing the ball on the "O" in the penalty box and "kick" it at the
opponent's goal, using your first finger and middle finger like a pair of legs.
You may draw soccer shoes onto your fingertips if you like.

SOCCER

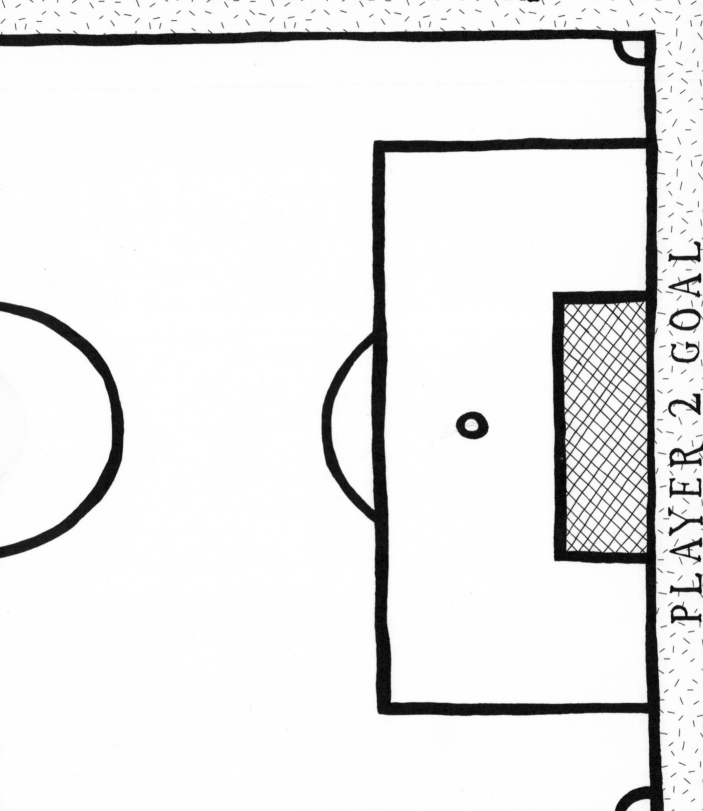

PLAYER 2 GOAL

The first player to score five goals is the winner! The ball MUST go into the crisscrossed area of the goal in order to count. Shooting from anywhere other than the "O" is a foul and results in a point being given to your opponent!

TREASURE HUNT

HOW TO PLAY

1. Hold this page up so you can't see each other's pictures—no cheating!

   Count down, "On your mark... Get set... Go!" On "Go," start searching for the objects listed on this page in your picture. When you find one, circle it.

2. The first player to find all the objects is the winner. If you think you have found all the objects, call out "Treasure found!" The other player can check your picture. If it turns out you have missed any, the other player automatically wins!!

3.

YOU MUST FIND:

A bow   A clothespin

A flower   A die

    A teddy   A nest
    bear

A tennis   A pair of
racket   scissors

    A watch

A rabbit   A pig

TREASURE HUNT

YOU MUST FIND:

A clothespin

A bow

A die

A flower

A teddy bear

A nest

A tennis racket

A pair of scissors

A watch

A pig

A rabbit

HOW TO PLAY

1. Hold this page up so you can't see each other's pictures—no cheating!

   Count down, "On your mark... Get set... Go!" On "Go," start searching for the objects

2. listed on this page in your picture. When you find one, circle it.

3. The first player to find all the objects is the winner. If you think you have found all the objects, call out "Treasure found!" The other player can check your picture. If it turns out you have missed any, the other player automatically wins!!

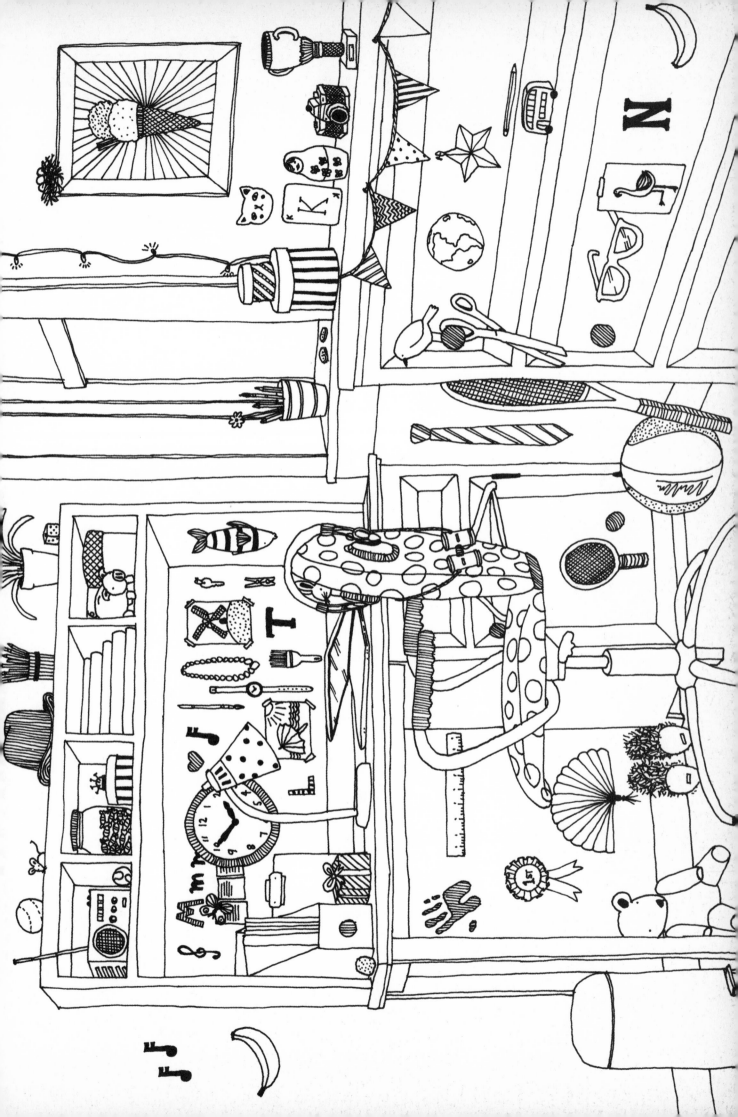

THE MIND-BL

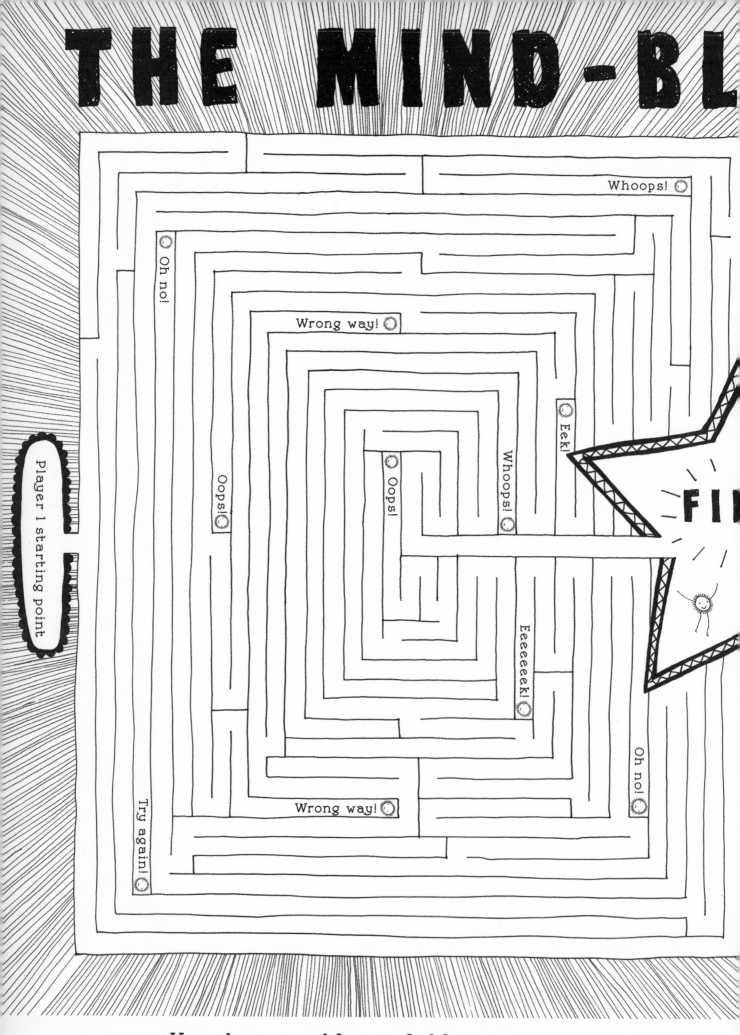

How to race through the maze . . .
Face each other at opposite sides of the book. See which player can get through the maze on his or her page and reach the center first.

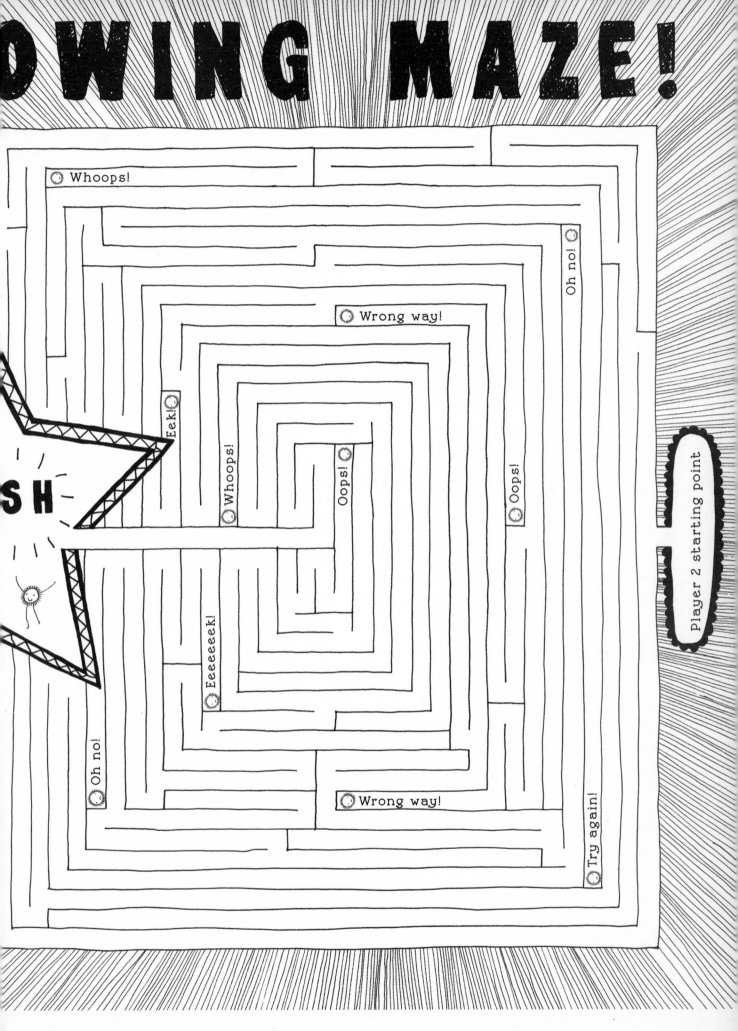

OWING MAZE!

The winner was

PLAY MORE
SQUARES
ON THIS PAGE

→

How to play . . .

Take turns drawing a single line to join any two
dots that are next to each other on the grid.
The lines can join the dots horizontally or
vertically (but not diagonally).

The player whose line completes one square earns
one point, puts his or her initials in that square
and gets another turn.

The game ends when no more lines can be drawn.
The player with the most points wins. This grid is
bigger than the first one, so you can score
more points!

  Good luck!

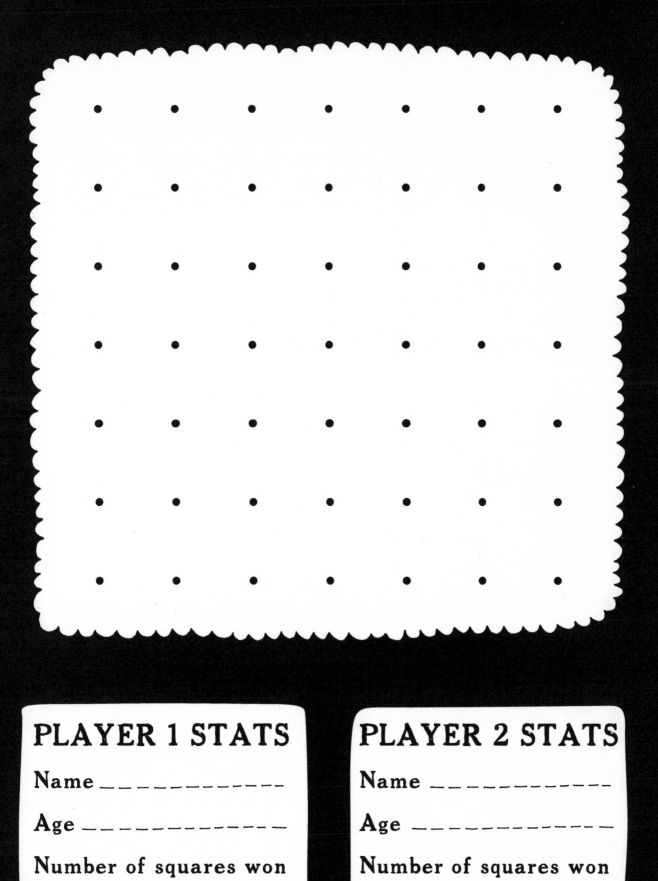

PLAYER 1 STATS

Name _ _ _ _ _ _ _ _ _ _ _ _

Age _ _ _ _ _ _ _ _ _ _ _ _ _

Number of squares won

_ _ _ _ _ _ _ _ _ _ _ _ _ _

PLAYER 2 STATS

Name _ _ _ _ _ _ _ _ _ _ _ _

Age _ _ _ _ _ _ _ _ _ _ _ _ _

Number of squares won

_ _ _ _ _ _ _ _ _ _ _ _ _ _

The winner was _ _ _ _ _ _ _ _ _ _ _ _ with _ _ _ squares.

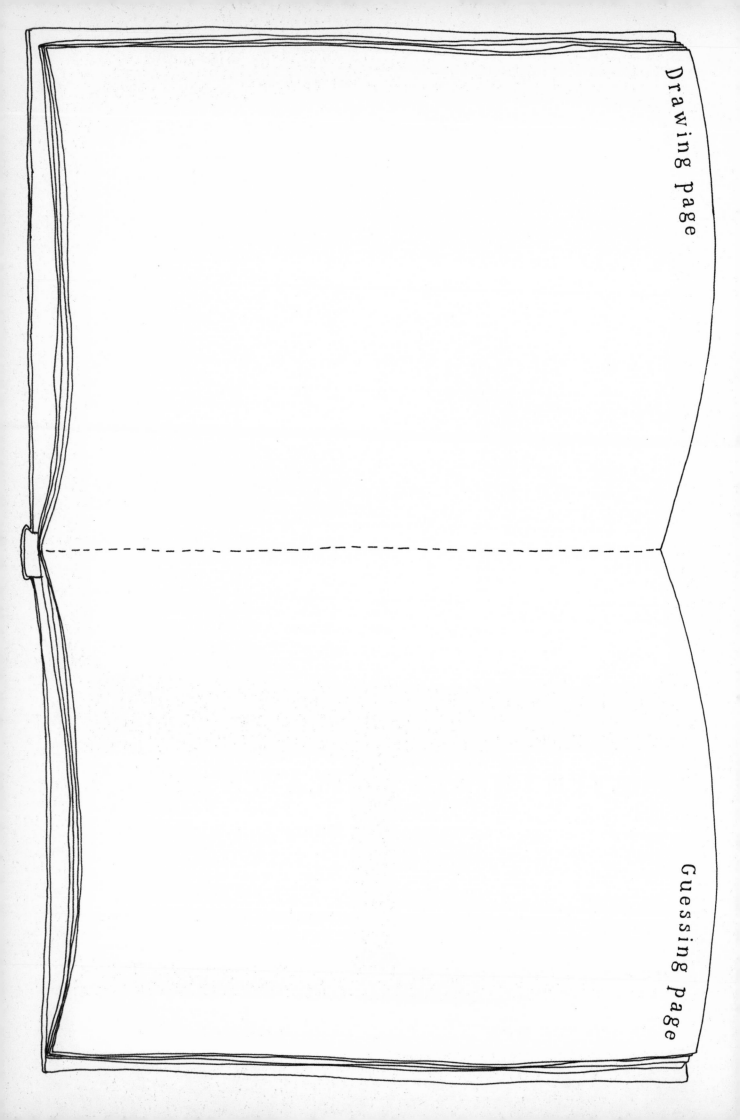

Drawing page

Guessing Page

SAY WHAT YOU SEE

—AGAIN!

With this page held up, Player 1 starts by drawing a picture on the drawing page.

Good work—but now the hard part!

Describe the shapes and lines that make up the picture, without saying what you have drawn. For example, if you drew a house you could describe it as a square with a triangle on top. Player 2 must try drawing a copy of it on the guessing page, just from the description.

No questions, and no guessing until the end!

To make it harder this time, set a timer and see if you can both complete your pictures in one minute.

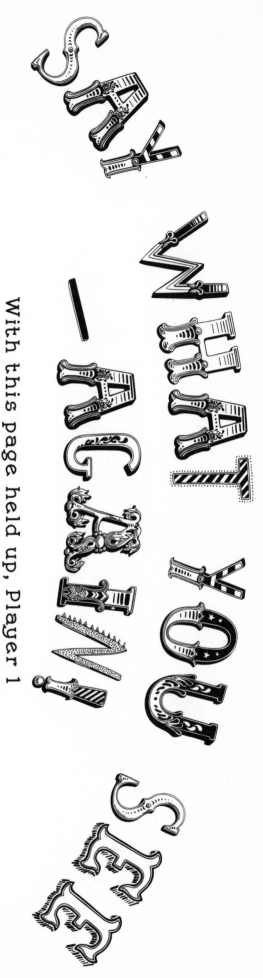

WHAT YOU SEE IS WHAT YOU DRAW AGAIN

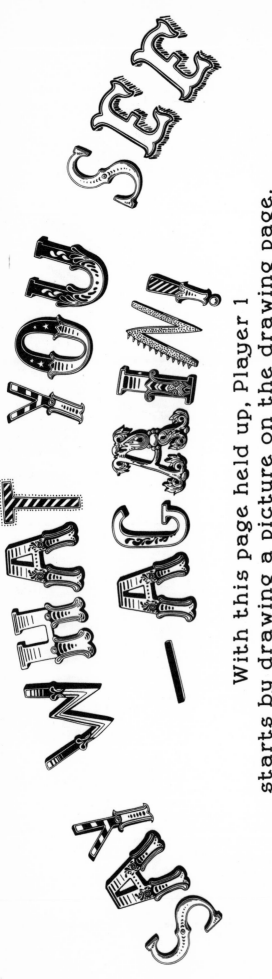

With this page held up, Player 1 starts by drawing a picture on the drawing page.

Good work—but now the hard part!

Describe the shapes and lines that make up the picture, without saying what you have drawn. For example, if you drew a house you could describe it as a square with a triangle on top. Player 2 must try drawing a copy of it on the guessing page, just from the description.

No questions, and no guessing until the end!

To make it harder this time, set a timer and see if you can both complete your pictures in one minute.

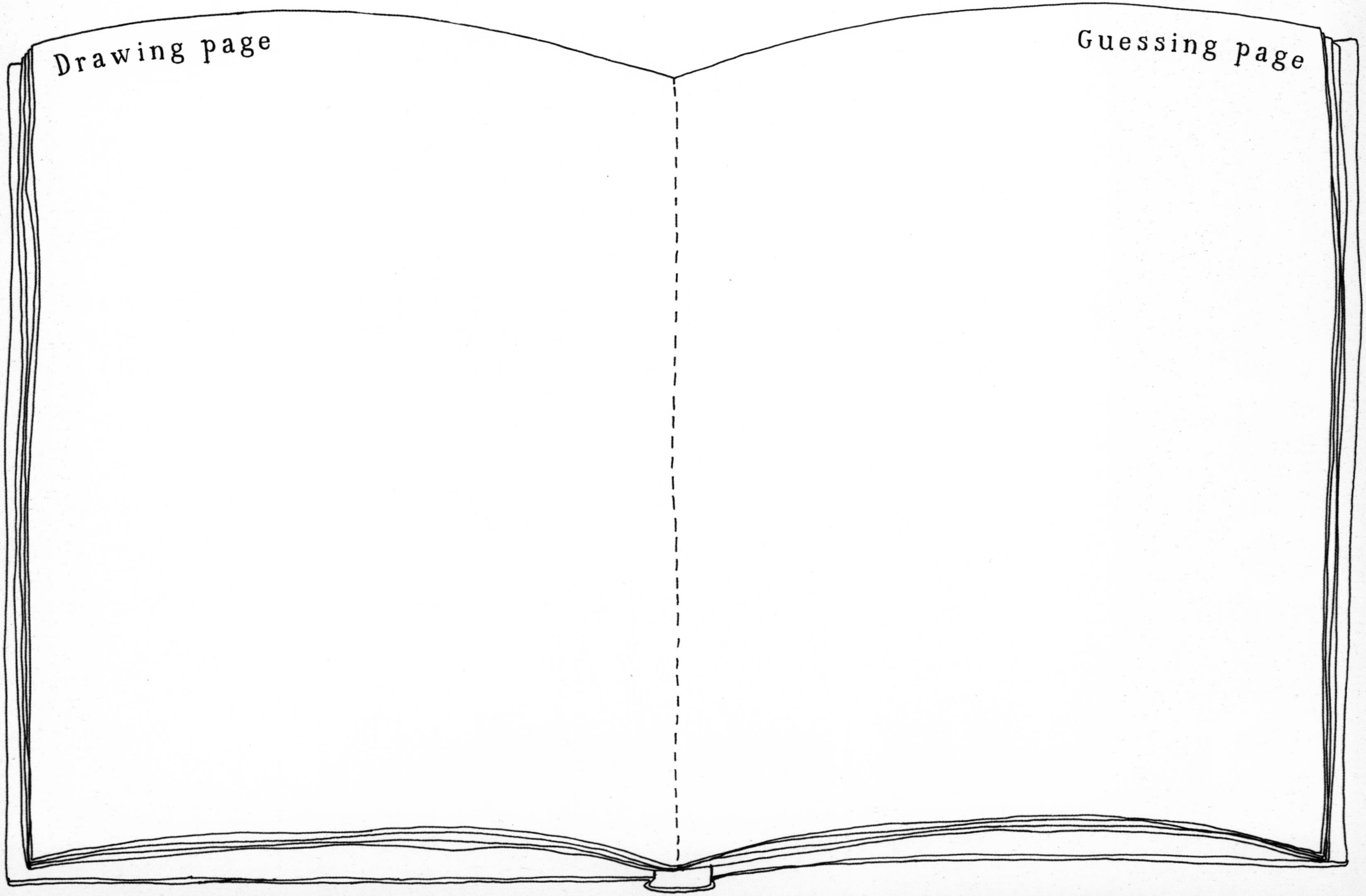

Guessing page

Drawing page

WHAT'S THE STORY? Part 2

PLAYER 1'S STORY

1 .... was a strange sort of

2 .... She lived in a

3 .... , for a start, and she was

also 4 .... , which made it hard to

5 .... She couldn't use a regular

6 .... so she had to

7 .... to school, 8 .... !

WORD KEY:

1. Female name	3. Noun	5. Verb	7. Verb
2. Noun	4. Adjective	6. Noun	8. Adverb (ending ... ly)

HOW IT WORKS . . .

Read through your story (silently!) and ask the other player for words to fill in the blanks (clues on the types of words you need are provided). Once you've both filled in all the blanks, take turns reading your story aloud to see whose is the funniest.

WORD TYPES

VERB – a doing word – walk, cook, jump...
NOUN – a naming word – house, giraffe, river...
ADJECTIVE – a describing word – green, tall, strange...
ADVERB – describes the way an action happens – slowly, completely, gently...
EXCLAMATION – a short utterance – Gosh! Hurray! Wow!

PLAYER 2'S STORY

On a visit to the zoo, 1 .... went to see the 2 ...., which were his favorite animals. They weren't in the enclosure, though, and a 3 .... anteater told him to look in the café. He went to the café, 4 ...., and found them all 5 .... a huge 6 .... for him! 7 "..................!" he shouted, as they all sat down to 8 ....

WORD KEY:

1. Boy's name
2. Noun (plural)
3. Adjective
4. Adverb (ending ...ly)
5. Verb (ending ...ing)
6. Noun
7. Exclamation!
8. Verb

MANDALA DRAWING

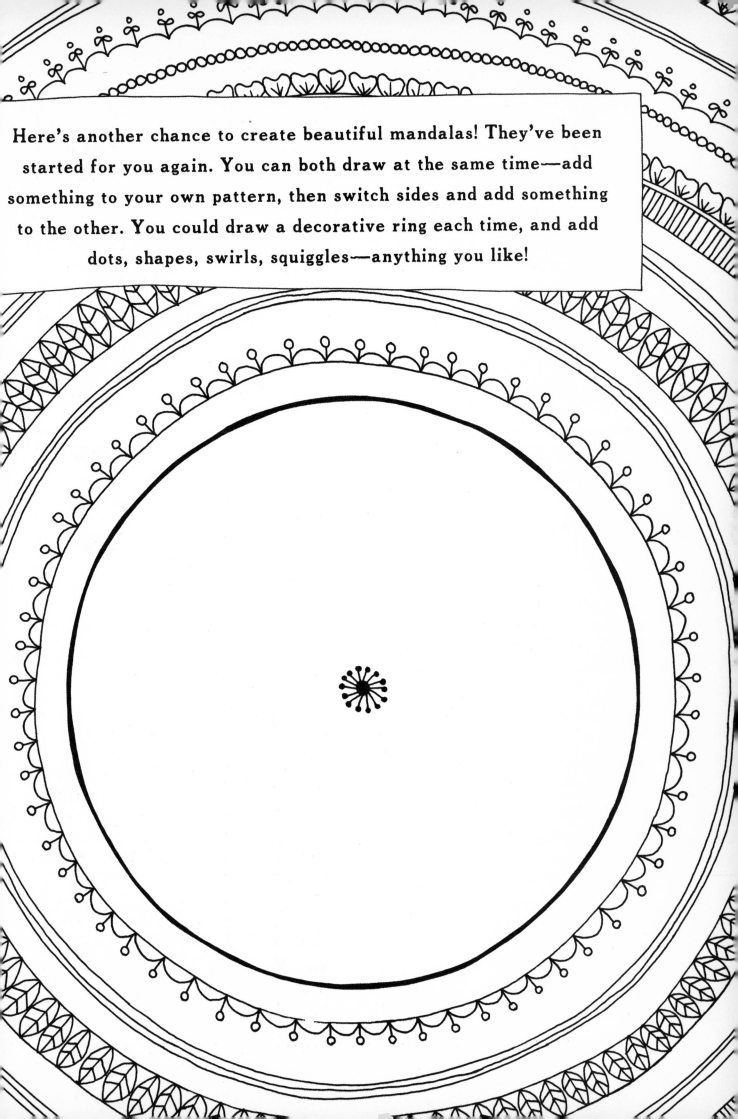

Here's another chance to create beautiful mandalas! They've been started for you again. You can both draw at the same time—add something to your own pattern, then switch sides and add something to the other. You could draw a decorative ring each time, and add dots, shapes, swirls, squiggles—anything you like!

MAIN GRID

Draw the fleet on this grid.

	1	2	3	4	5	6	7	8	9	10	11	12
A												
B												
C												
D												
E												
F												
G												
H												
I												
J												
K												
L												

THE FLEET

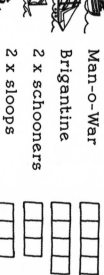

Man-o-War

Brigantine

2 x schooners

2 x sloops

TRACKING GRID

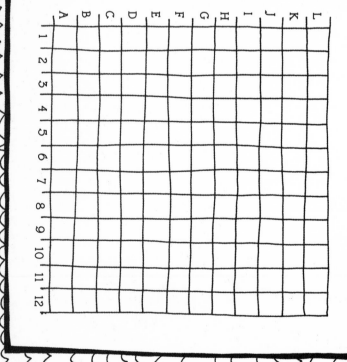

	1	2	3	4	5	6	7	8	9	10	11	12
A												
B												
C												
D												
E												
F												
G												
H												
I												
J												
K												
L												

SINK THE PIRATE SHIP

HOW TO PLAY . . .

With this page held up, choose where you want each boat in your pirate fleet to be. Shade in the correct number of squares on the main grid for each boat, then you're ready to play.

Take turns in calling out a square from the grid (A3, D5, etc.). If the other player has a boat on a square you call out, you've got a hit. Mark hits with a cross on the tracking grid, and misses with a dash. This will help you build a picture of where the other player's fleet is located.

Once you've guessed all of the squares taken up by one boat, you have SUNK THE PIRATE SHIP—Arrrr! When all of one player's boats have been sunk, the game is over and the other player wins.

SINK THE PIRATE SHIP

HOW TO PLAY . . . .

With this page held up, choose where you want each boat in the pirate fleet to be. Shade in the correct number of squares on the main grid for each boat, then you're ready to play.

Take turns in calling out a square from the grid (A3, D5, etc.). If the other player has a boat on a square you call out, you've got a hit. Mark hits with a cross on the tracking grid, and misses with a dash. This will help you build a picture of where the other player's fleet is located.

Once you've guessed all of the squares taken up by one boat, you have SUNK THE PIRATE SHIP—Arrrr! When all of one player's boats have been sunk, the game is over and the other player wins.

THE FLEET

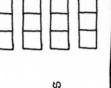

 Man-o-War

 Brigantine

 2 x schooners

2 x sloops

TRACKING GRID

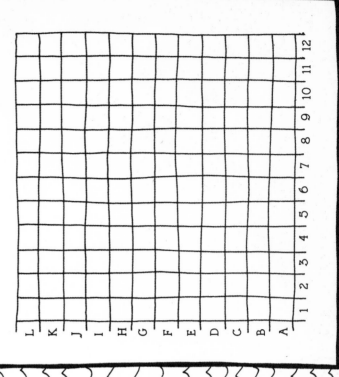

MAIN GRID

Draw the fleet on this grid.

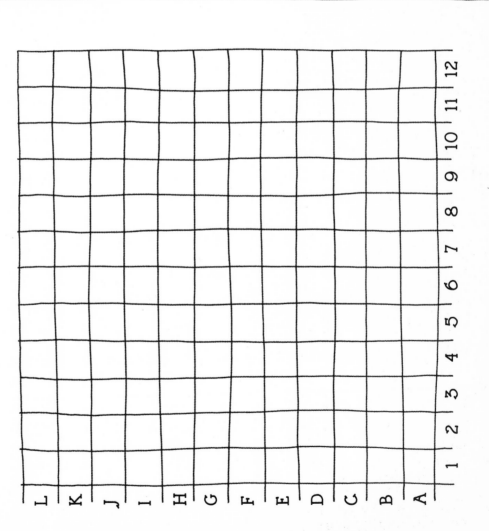

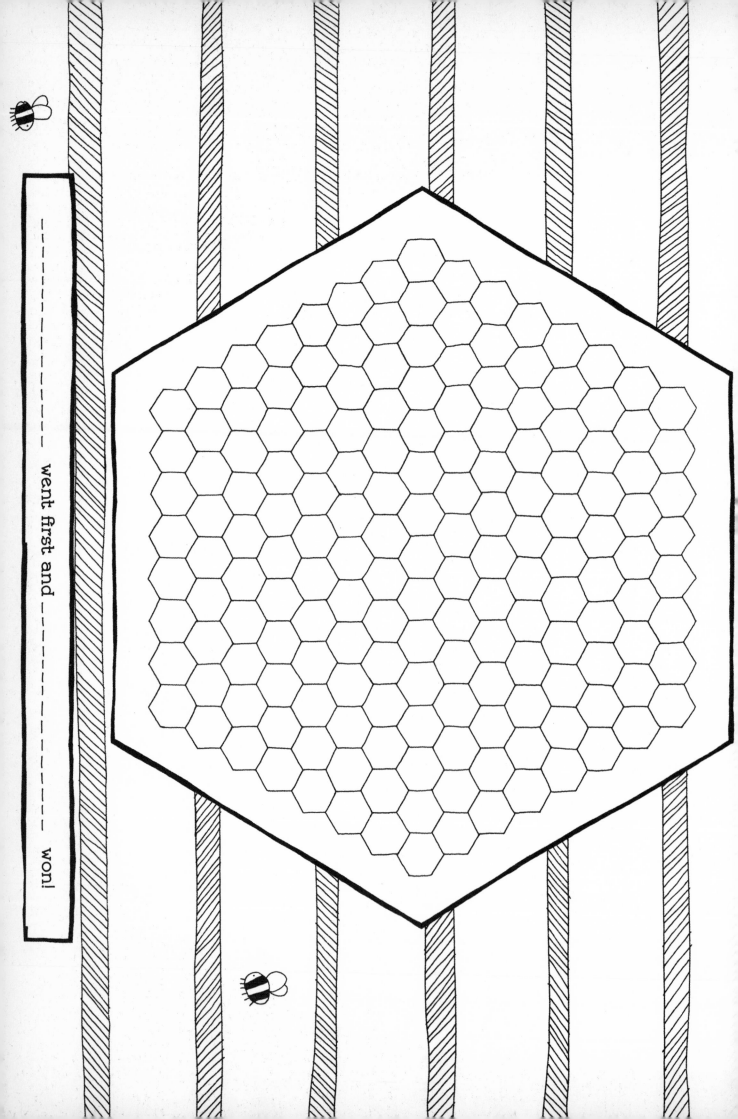

_____ went first and _____ won!

HEXAGONS 2

HOW TO PLAY . . .

Each player should choose a colored pencil to use for the game. Take turns filling one "cell" of the board at a time with your color.

The goal is coloring cells next to each other to create one of these three connections:

1. A ring, which is a continuous loop with at least one cell in the middle.

2. A fork, which connects three edges of the board (the corners don't count as an edge).

3. A bridge, which connects any two of the corners.

Raise the stakes by trying to complete the game within three minutes.

MY SCORE WAS:

MY LIST OF WORDS FOUND:

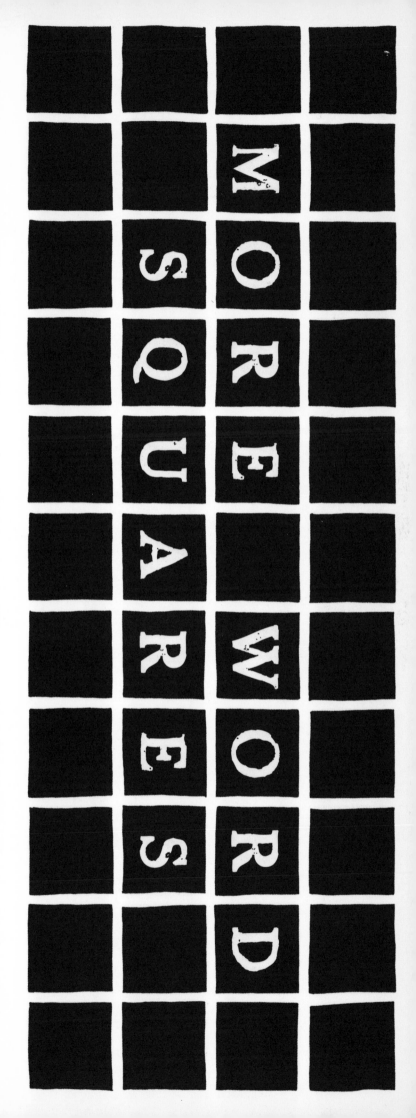

As before, take turns calling out letters and writing them in the grids. The goal is to arrange the letters as you write them down to make as many words as possible . . .

Once both grids are full, mark down all the words you can find, and figure out your scores. You get points for words in a vertical or horizontal row (not diagonals):

6-letter word—Amazing! 15 points!
5-letter word—Wow, well done! 10 points!
4-letter word—Good effort, 5 points.
3-letter word—Not bad, 2 points.
2-letter word—All right, 1 point.

This time, once the grids are full, you have just three minutes to find all the words!

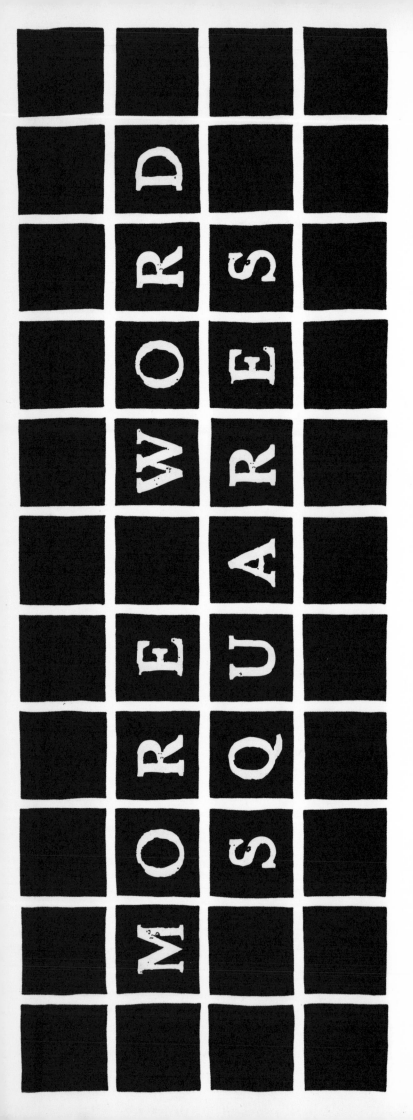

As before, take turns calling out letters and writing them in the grids. The goal is to arrange the letters as you write them down to make as many words as possible . . . .

Once both grids are full, mark down all the words you can find, and figure out your scores. You get points for words in a vertical or horizontal row (not diagonals):

6-letter word—Amazing, 15 points!
5-letter word—Wow, well done! 10 points!
4-letter word—Good effort, 5 points.
3-letter word—Not bad, 2 points.
2-letter word—All right, 1 point.

This time, once the grids are full, you have just three minutes to find all the words!

MY LIST OF WORDS FOUND:

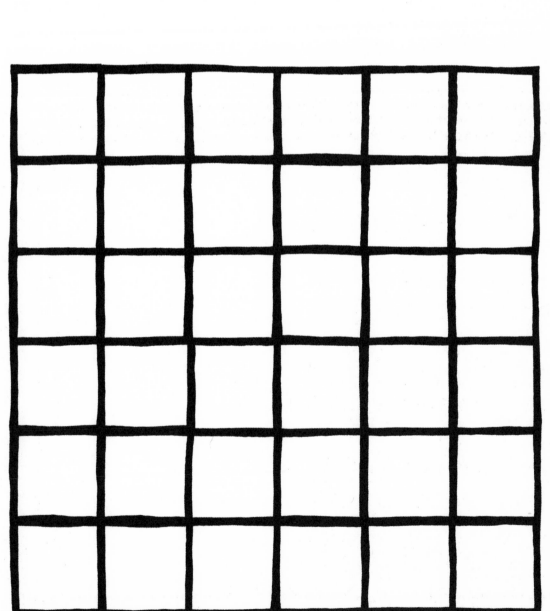

MY SCORE WAS:

SQUIGGL

Run out of ideas for new pictures again? No problem!

Do a quick squiggle in the middle of the frame,
then turn the book around.

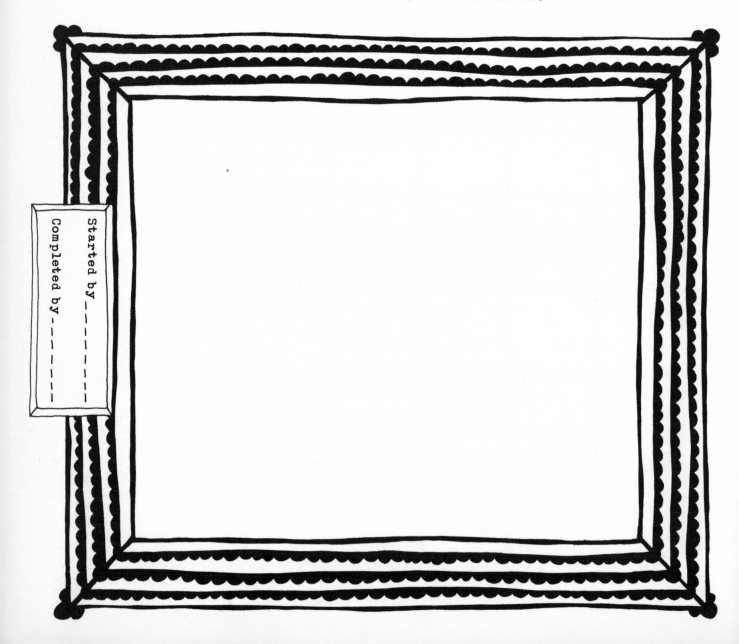

Started by _ _ _ _ _ _ _
Completed by _ _ _ _ _ _

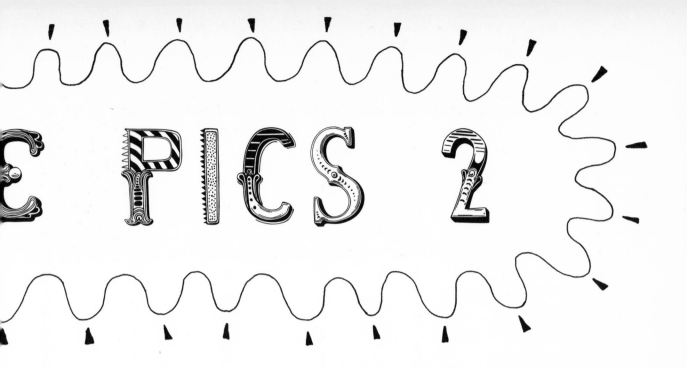

PICS 2

Now that the other player has started the drawing, you can see what you think it looks like and turn it into a complete work of art.

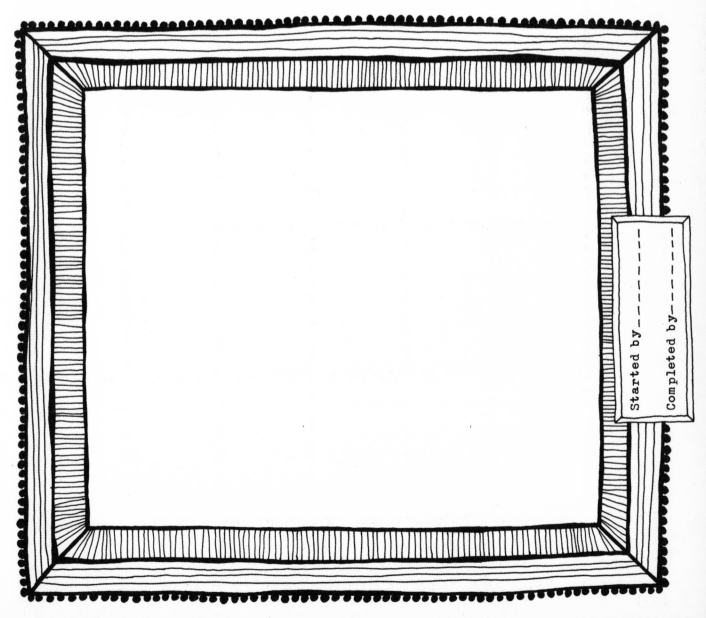

Started by ------

Completed by ------

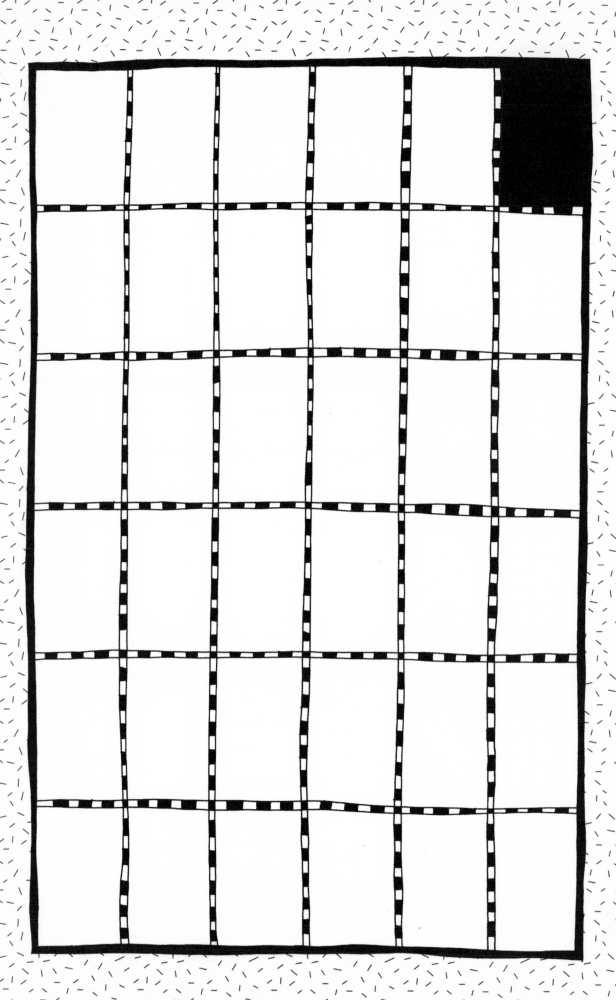

MY TOTAL CATEGORIES SCORE WAS: _____

CATEGORIES 2

How does it work?

1. This time you can choose your own categories and keyword. Write a category at the top of each column.

Then, choose a five-letter keyword and write it down the left side of each player's grid, so that each letter is at the start of one row. Both grids need to have the same keyword and categories, in the same order.

2. Hold up this page, set a timer for four minutes—and you're ready!

In each square, write a word that fits under the category at the top of the column and starts with the letter at the beginning of the row.

3. Compare your answers and make sure you agree the words are OK (no made-up words!). You get no points for words that both you and the other player wrote down, but one point per word that only you thought of. If you filled the whole grid, you get five bonus points.

The game is finished when the time is up, or when one player fills the grid completely.

The player with the most points wins!

TIPS:

You can choose any five categories, and any five-letter keyword (as long as it does not contain repeated letters—and it's best to avoid Q, X, and Z, unless you want a BIG challenge or a long game!). Here are some suggestions to get you started:

Categories:	Keywords:
– Cities	– REACH
– Birds	– BENCH
– Foods	– BLADE
– Flowers	– GLIDE
– Vehicles	– CANDY
– Body parts	– TABLE
– Toys	– BEARS
– Insects	– LAUGH
– Buildings	– HOUND

CATEGORIES 2

How does it work?

1. This time you can choose your own categories and keyword. Write a category at the top of each column. Then, choose a five-letter keyword and write it down the left side of each player's grid, so that each letter is at the start of one row. Both the grids need to have the same keyword and categories, in the same order.

2. Hold up this page, set a timer for four minutes—and you're ready!

In each square, write a word that fits under the category at the top of the column, and starts with the letter at the beginning of the row.

The game is finished when the time is up, or when one player fills the grid completely.

3. Compare your answers and make sure you agree the words are OK (no made-up words!). You get no points for words that both you and the other player wrote down, but one point per word that only you thought of. If you filled the whole grid, you get five bonus points.

The player with the most points wins!

TIPS:

You can choose any five categories, and any five-letter keyword (as long as it does not contain repeated letters—and it's best to avoid Q, X, and Z, unless you want a BIG challenge or a long game!). Here are some suggestions to get you started:

Categories:
- Cities
- Birds
- Types of food
- Flowers
- Vehicles
- Body parts
- Toys
- Insects
- Buildings

Keywords:
- REACH
- BENCH
- BLADE
- GLIDE
- CANDY
- TABLE
- BEARS
- LAUGH
- HOUND

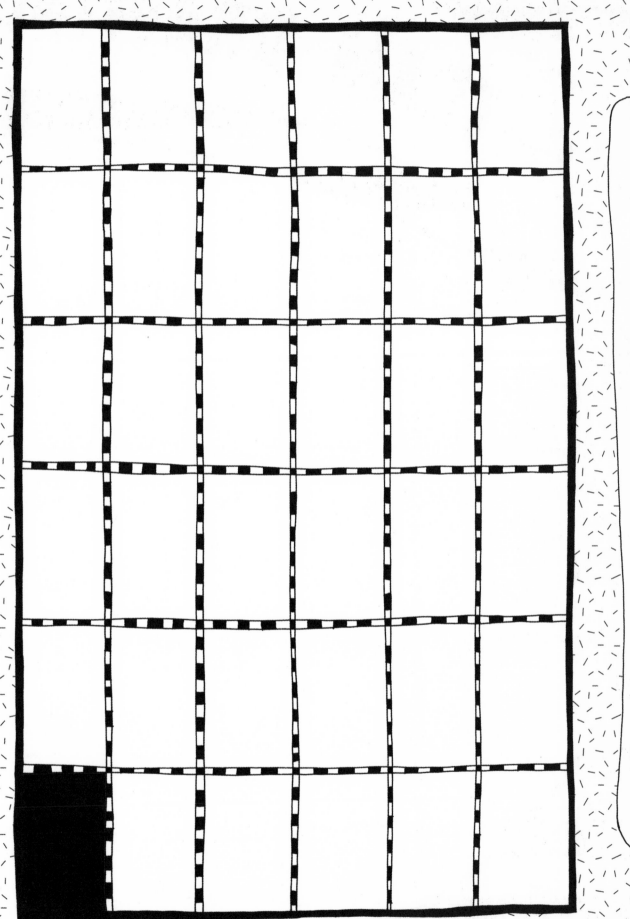

MY TOTAL CATEGORIES SCORE WAS: - - - - - -

TAG-TEAM DRAWING

Make a super-speedy sketch with another game of tag-team drawing, against the clock. Set a timer for two minutes—when it starts player 1 does a quick, simple doodle, then rotates the paper 90 degrees. Player 2 then adds to the doodle, and rotates the paper another 90 degrees. Keep taking turns until you're out of time... Keep it quick!!

HOW TO
PLAY:

One player plays with black dots, the
other plays with white dots.

Take turns connecting the dots, one line
at a time. You can connect up or across
(not diagonally), and you can only
connect dots of your own color. You
cannot cross a line that has
already been drawn.

The goal is to connect the dots in your
color to make a continuous line
(or pipe) between the shorter sides
of the grid.

L A Y E R

- ● Black dot player's name _ _ _ _ _ _ _ _ _ _ _ _ _ _ _
- ○ White dot player's name _ _ _ _ _ _ _ _ _ _ _ _ _

◄ - - - - - White dot player joins side to side - - - ►

Black dot player joins up or down

The winner was _ _ _ _ _ _ _ _ _ _ _ _ _ _

SPOT THE DIFFERENCES RACE

Race each other to find the ten differences between these pictures—circle them as you find them. The first player to find all ten, wins.

Hold this page up—and no peeking!

SPOT THE DIFFFERENCES RACE

Race each other to find the ten differences between these pictures—circle them as you find them. The first player to find all ten, wins.

Hold this page up—and no peeking!

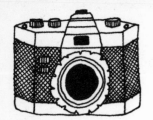

PICTURE

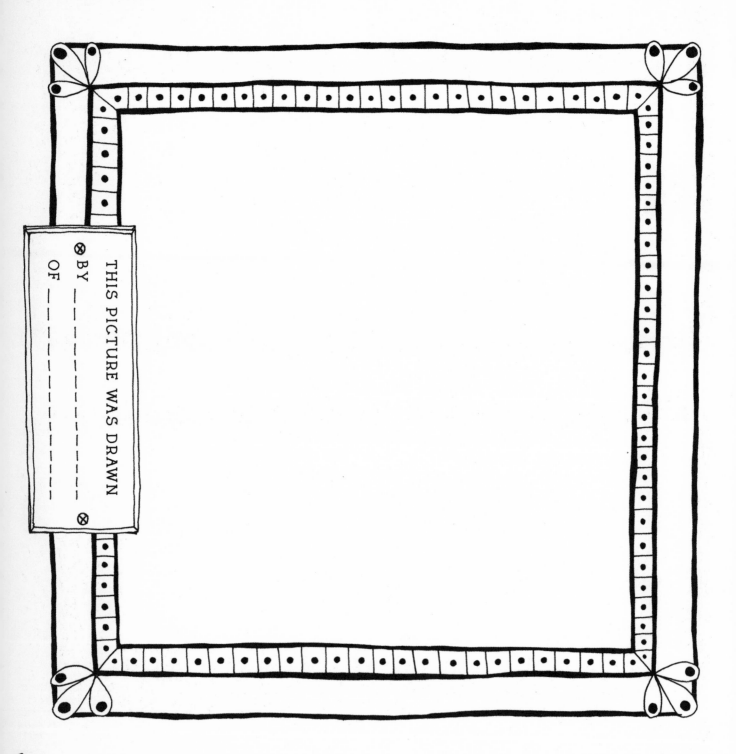

THIS PICTURE WAS DRAWN

⊗ BY
————————————
————————————
OF
————————————
————————————
⊗

Another chance to draw a portrait of your friend.
HOWEVER, this time you must hold the pencil in
your non-dominant hand.

PERFECT 2

THIS PICTURE WAS DRAWN

BY _ _ _ _ _ _ _ _ _

OF _ _ _ _ _ _ _ _ _

Yes, if you're right-handed, it's time to try with the left, and if you're left-handed, switch to the right. Tricky...

MORE SPROUTS!

Sprouts is like a game of dot-to-dot,
but with a twist . . .

Here's how it works:

Starting with the three dots on the opposite page,
take turns drawing a line to connect two dots
(or the line may start and end on the same dot).
You should also draw a new dot somewhere on
the new line.

Lines cannot cross, and each dot can only have
three lines sprouting out of it. Eventually, it will
become impossible to draw a new line without
crossing an existing one—the last player to
draw a line wins!

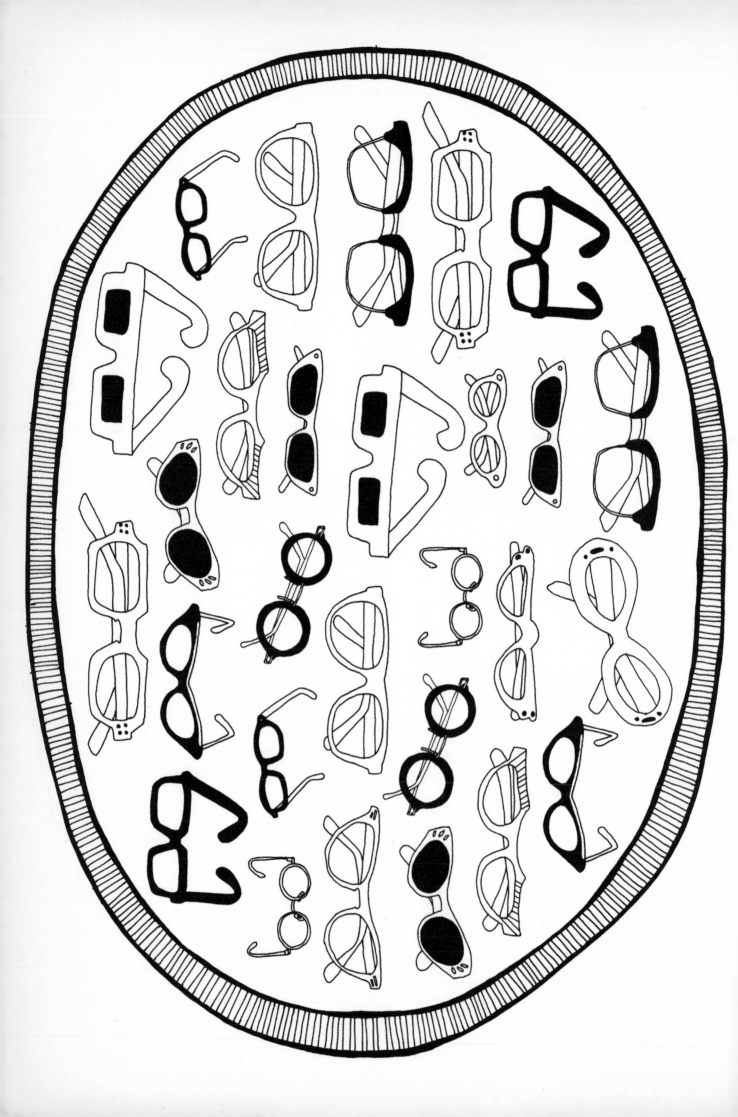

FIND THE PAIRS RACE

How it works:

Hidden in this scene are 12 pairs of identical glasses.

Starting at the same time, try to find the pairs and draw a line connecting them as you find them—the first to find all 12, wins!

FIND THE PAIRS RACE

How it works:

Hidden in this scene are 12 pairs of identical glasses. Starting at the same time, try to find the pairs and draw a line connecting them as you find them—the first to find all 12, wins!

Hold up this page

MIRROR DRAWING 2

drew this picture

Another chance to play artist and student... The artist begins drawing in one frame, while the student must exactly mirror the drawing at the same time to create a perfect mirror image.

drew this picture

Another chance to play artist and student... The artist begins drawing in one frame, while the student must exactly mirror the drawing at the same time to create a perfect mirror image.

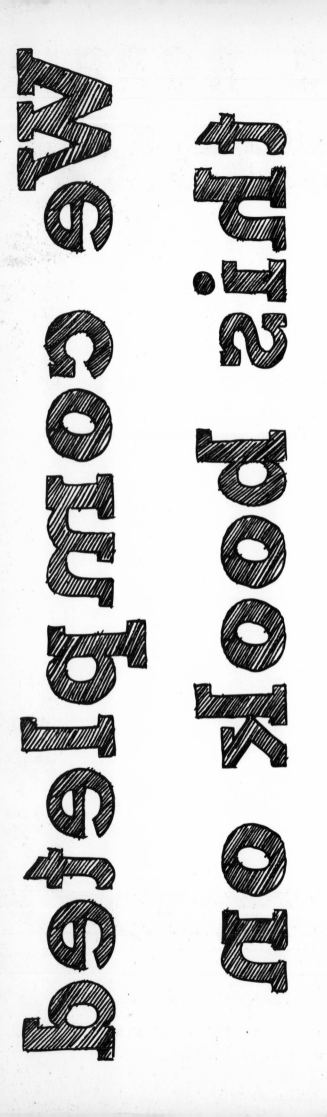

Hold this page up to a mirror and then write your completion date below (make sure the writing is back-to-front, too).